China and the United States as Aid Donors

Past and Future Trajectories

About the East-West Center

The East-West Center promotes better relations and understanding among the people and nations of the United States, Asia, and the Pacific through cooperative study, research, and dialogue. Established by the US Congress in 1960, the Center serves as a resource for information and analysis on critical issues of common concern, bringing people together to exchange views, build expertise, and develop policy options.

The Center's 21-acre Honolulu campus, adjacent to the University of Hawai'i at Mānoa, is located midway between Asia and the US mainland and features research, residential, and international conference facilities. The Center's Washington, DC, office focuses on preparing the United States for an era of growing Asia Pacific prominence.

The Center is an independent, public, nonprofit organization with funding from the US government, and additional support provided by private agencies, individuals, foundations, corporations, and governments in the region.

Policy Studies
an East-West Center series

Series Editors
Dieter Ernst and Marcus Mietzner

Description
Policy Studies presents original research on pressing economic and political policy challenges for governments and industry across Asia, and for the region's relations with the United States. Written for the policy and business communities, academics, journalists, and the informed public, the peer-reviewed publications in this series provide new policy insights and perspectives based on extensive fieldwork and rigorous scholarship.

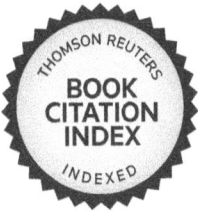

Policy Studies is indexed in the *Web of Science Book Citation Index*. The *Web of Science* is the largest and most comprehensive citation index available.

Notes to Contributors
Submissions may take the form of a proposal or complete manuscript. For more information on the Policy Studies series, please contact the Series Editors.

Editors, Policy Studies
East-West Center
1601 East-West Road
Honolulu, Hawai'i 96848-1601
Tel: 808.944.7197
Publications@EastWestCenter.org
EastWestCenter.org/PolicyStudies

Policy
Studies | 77

China and the United States as Aid Donors
Past and Future Trajectories

Patrick Kilby

China and the United States as Aid Donors: Past and Future Trajectories
Patrick Kilby

ISSN 1547-1349 (print) and 1547-1330 (electronic)
ISBN 978-0-86638-282-3 (print) and 978-0-86638-283-0 (electronic)

The views expressed are those of the author(s) and not necessarily those of the East-West Center.

Print copies are available from Amazon.com. Free electronic copies of most titles are available on the East-West Center website, at EastWestCenter.org/PolicyStudies, where submission guidelines can also be found. Questions about the series should be directed to:

Publications Office
East-West Center
1601 East-West Road
Honolulu, Hawai'i 96848-1601

Telephone: 808.944.7197

EWCBooks@EastWestCenter.org
EastWestCenter.org/PolicyStudies

Contents

Executive Summary

The United States and China have followed nearly parallel paths as providers of foreign aid over the past seven decades. Although these programs were ostensibly aimed at Third World economic development, both China and the United States have leveraged their aid programs to further their own national interests, but have used very different strategies. The United States has largely provided foreign aid with the aim of stabilizing the world order and to advance its interests, initially as part of a broader Cold War strategy and more recently as part of its War on Terror. Its approach has been to develop patron-client relationships with recipient countries, using aid to build alliances and

China and the US have used their aid programs for their own national interests, but have used very different strategies

promote economic and political liberalization. The Trump administration has now proposed cutting foreign aid by up to one-third in favor of an "America first" policy.

China, on the other hand, has used its foreign aid program primarily to strengthen its position as a leader of the Global South, with a hands-off political approach, emphasizing reciprocity and solidarity with its foreign aid recipients. At the same time as the United States cuts its aid program, the Chinese government is ramping up its own foreign aid and investment programs. For example, the Belt Road Initiative (BRI) is supported with a Chinese government commitment of $40b to the Silk Road Fund to expand both overland and maritime trade links of China with Europe, Central and South Asia, and Africa.

This is not a new direction for China, but rather an articulation of a further step in a constant trajectory that this study explores. China's foreign aid program had its beginnings with Chinese Premier Zhou Enlai's entrance on the global stage at the Asian-African Conference at Bandung, Indonesia, in April 1955. This conference saw the political leadership from 29 developing countries come together over a week to look beyond the Cold War alliances they were part of and map out a path for an assertive voice from the Global South. The first clause of the Bandung declaration called for increased South-South "...economic cooperation on the basis of mutual interest and respect for national sovereignty." China took this call to heart and commenced a program of foreign aid starting with Egypt in 1956 and expanding into the rest of Africa and Asia.

This is quite different from the US aid trajectory, which this study argues had its origins in the Cold War with aid to Greece and Turkey in early 1947 to prevent them falling into the Soviet camp, and from there was used to build anti-Soviet alliances. Despite President Truman's Point Four Program of 1949 for increased foreign aid for development, a skeptical Congress kept aid volumes low and tied aid to the Cold War security agenda of the Eisenhower administration. The Kennedy administration moved beyond the focus on security and matching Soviet efforts, introducing a development agenda for the "free world" based on promoting free market capitalism and opposing state-led development. This was despite the economic successes of the state-led policies of Japan and South Korea, and later China. With the end of the Cold War in 1989, the focus of the US aid program shifted to democratization under President Clinton. Under George W. Bush, after the September 11 attacks, it was expanded to support the War on Terror.

This study tracks the development of Chinese aid since the 1970s when it was reaching over 70 countries and, most notably, constructing the TAZARA railway, a flagship project of 2,000km linking the copper mines of Zambia to Tanzanian ports, thus bypassing the colonial remnants of Rhodesia and South Africa. With this one project China made an unambiguous statement of solidarity with the Global South.

After a hiatus in the 1980s when China's own rapid growth was given priority, its aid program increased in the 1990s following the Tiananmen Square violent crackdown and the associated condemnation of China from the West. Here the focus was not only on building solidarity, but also trade and investment linkages as well. In the 2010s, there has been a further expansion of China's foreign aid with the BRI program aimed at building closer economic and trade relationships across Asia and making use of excess capacity in Chinese industry.

The study concludes with a discussion of the West's reduced leverage, not only in promoting globalization and the broader neoliberal agenda, but also in the broader liberal regime around social justice, gender justice, human rights, environmental norms, and other hard-won global agreements. The influence of the United States is being challenged by China, which has been using its foreign aid to expand its global influence in ways that are quite different from the United States and the West. The question is how will the United States, and the West more broadly, respond to this challenge in a time of deep aid cuts and in the context of rising nationalism and more authoritarian states that are increasingly rejecting the post-war liberal world order.

China and the United States as Aid Donors
Past and Future Trajectories

Introduction

The Trump administration's 2018 budget proposes to cut US foreign aid by one third, making it the largest cut in foreign aid since the end of the Cold War. It also comes at a time when China is using its aid program and other official flows to assert its influence across Asia and Africa, most recently with its Belt Road Initiative. For the United States to cut its aid program so drastically at this critical juncture will effectively cede the field to China after a decades-long "aid race" in which each vied for influence in the Global South using the "soft power" of foreign aid. An exploration of this history will shed light on why a continued and strong foreign aid engagement with the Global South is important.

First, it will be useful to map the origins of both foreign aid programs and show how they developed up to the 1980s. An important aspect of this is China's development leadership of the Global South, particularly in the 1970s when the West was challenged by UNCTAD, the New International Economic Order, and more assertive Southern voices. The 1990s and the 2000s saw China cement its political solidarity relationships with economic ones at a time when the United States largely ignored China and focused on democratization (mainly in Eastern Europe) and the War on Terror. This discussion provides an important background for a discussion of how the Trump administration's aid cuts limit the use of the US aid program in better engaging with China and the Global South to strengthen and advance some of the liberal values that are under threat by rising nationalism. Instead, China's hands-off approach to bilateral relations will go unchallenged in an era of growing authoritarianism.

An Overview

The rise of the United States and China as foreign aid donors, the United States from the mid-1940s and China from the mid-1950s, followed surprisingly similar paths but with some important differences. While the United States as a modern bilateral donor[1] had its origins in the immediate post–World War II context, with an aid program to Turkey and Greece in 1947, and President Truman's Point Four Program in 1949, the US aid program did not increase substantially until the mid-1950s when the Soviet Union started a foreign aid race to build alliances to complement the arms race. Similarly, until the late 1980s the US program was an adjunct to the Cold War, and the foreign aid program complemented the US security strategy by developing and cementing Cold War alliances. In the early 2000s the US aid program expanded again with its focus on the War on Terror.

For China, the Asian-African Conference in Bandung, Indonesia, in April 1955 marked its first step in establishing a foreign aid program beyond support for its immediate communist neighbors. Bandung was also the first step by developing countries, acting as a collective group, in articulating their own development cooperation agenda, marking the beginning of South-South cooperation. China immediately took up the challenge, beginning a foreign aid program to Egypt in 1956.

The Chinese aid program, after a few halting steps in the 1960s, grew rapidly from the early 1970s until it stabilized in the 1980s, then grew rapidly again from the 1990s until the present day. From the 1990s, the focus of the Chinese program shifted from cementing political and diplomatic relationships to more direct economic cooperation to build strategic partnerships, culminating in the 2010s with the Belt Road Initiative (BRI) across Asia and Africa, using a mix of foreign aid, other official flows, and foreign direct investment (FDI).

For both the United States and China, their foreign aid programs, while ostensibly about Third World economic development, were very much driven by their respective national interests. For the US, Cold War rivalry meant that building alliances and protecting allies was a central part of its aid program in its early years. For China, it was a pathway to regaining its status as a respected voice on the global stage after what Zhou Enlai in the 1950s referred to as the "century of humiliation," and then to building economic ties to realize Xi Jinping's China Dream, a reference to China's former glory.

> *Both foreign aid programs were very much driven by their respective national interests*

The strategies adopted by China and the US, however, were very different. The United States adopted more of a patron-client relationship with its aid recipients, which included their adoption of free market capitalist economic systems and, from the late 1980s, broader democratic principles in their political systems. While the United States did give aid to communist countries from the outset, most notably to Yugoslavia in 1949, it tended to promote economic and political liberalization among its allies and aid partners. China, on the other hand, was less interested in the nature or the economic approaches of the partner government, but rather emphasized solidarity in developing its long-term political and economic relationships. While these often were around developing trade and investment relationships, this was not always the case, as increasing China's status as a leader of the Global South was also important. The only political condition China placed on its development partners was support of a One China Policy, restricting official recognition of Taiwan. It was not until the 2000s that a China-based model of development, the so-called Beijing Consensus, was articulated. It focused on filling both soft and hard infrastructure needs, for improved connectivity within and across Asia and Africa.

China's programs, like those of the US, were global in nature, but focused on Africa until after the Cold War, when China increased its focus on South, Central, and West Asia. There was less historical baggage in building relationships with Africa than with many of the countries in Asia, and with over 50 independent, mostly nonaligned countries, Africa could have a more united voice. Asia during the Cold War was more politically divided, with many countries allied with either the Soviet Union or the US.

The Origins of US Foreign Aid Programs

The US foreign aid program can be traced back to the early part of the nineteenth century, with the Monroe Doctrine that built on notions of manifest destiny and American exceptionalism in its expansion westward into the Pacific and southward into Latin America (Picard and Buss 2009; Coles 2002; Zoysa 2005). These ideas, Zoysa argues, have their origins in the values and Puritan beliefs of the first European settlers to arrive in Plymouth, MA in 1620. The United States sent technical missions abroad from the 1830s onwards, and by the 1870s a number of foreign governments turned directly to the United States for aid. However, until the 1940s, the focus was mainly on Latin America and flagship projects such as the Inter-American Highway of the 1920s, and some development programs in the Philippines in the 1920s and 1930s (Picard and Buss 2009; Liska 1960).

In the 1940s the focus was on reconstruction following the devastation of World War II, which would be led by the nascent World Bank in concert with the International Monetary Fund, which had oversight of the global financial system (Lavelle 2013; Engel 2012; Caufield 1996). This vision quickly unraveled when the Soviet Union took a more belligerent approach to the political rehabilitation of Europe, and effectively annexed much of Eastern Europe, setting up Soviet-style governments in those countries (Koslowski and Kratochwil 1994; Vieira 2016). In 1946, communist insurgencies in Greece, as well as Soviet pressure on Turkey for disputed territory and unfettered maritime access to the Mediterranean Sea, threatened both governments. If these strategies were successful and Greece and Turkey moved into the Soviet orbit, the West's Middle East allies and its oil supply would be threatened. In early 1947, the UK, which was too financially strapped to provide support to Greece and Turkey, asked the United States to supply economic and military aid. This first postwar US foreign aid program led to the Truman Doctrine of 1947, which rejected US isolationism in favor of containing communist aggression (Tansky 1967; United States Congress 1957a, 1957b; Picard and Buss 2009; Lancaster 2008; Morley and Morley 1961).

Following the provision of economic and military support to Greece and Turkey, the Truman government expanded the foreign aid program to the rest of Europe and beyond, but this time with a developmental rather than a military objective. While Truman's Point Four Program of 1949 still tied the foreign aid into a broader framework of security, it also introduced the idea that "…trade and civilisation were inseparable" (Caufield 1996, 48).[2] The themes of Point Four were "poverty, economic growth, and democracy and freedom against Soviet Communism" (Picard and Buss 2009, 88). Even though the aid from the US Point Four Program was to be in the form of technical assistance rather than large-scale grants or loans (Picard and Buss 2009; Wood 1986), it only passed Congress by one vote (Wood 1986). This was an early demonstration of the ambivalence the US Congress continues to have for foreign aid (Hagen and Ruttan 1988). Around the same time, Marshal Tito of Yugoslavia split from Stalin, and after much soul searching the United States provided its first foreign aid (including military aid) to a communist state in 1949, largely without conditions (Lees 1978; Liska 1960).

The Marshall Plan, however, was set up to be separate from the foreign aid program and aimed at: rebuilding Western Europe and Japan as a group of US allies to contain communism; stimulating the US economy via increased industrial exports to Europe; and accessing raw materials from developing countries through their European patrons (Wood 1986; Morley and Morley 1961; Hagen and Ruttan 1988). The Marshall Plan thus resulted in large flows to developing countries from their colonial powers (Picard and Buss 2009). In addition, the Marshall Plan and the US aid program had an ideological agenda of not only containing communism, but also challenging the statism and national capitalism that prevailed through much of Western Europe (Loayza 2003; Wood 1986). Wood argues that this "has been the real threat economic aid has been used to counter rather than communism" (Wood 1986 66). The anti-statist agenda has been a continuing implicit, if not explicit, objective of the US aid program ever since. The Marshall Plan, however, had limited success in pressuring European governments away from state-led economic recovery, and what the United States saw as stifling regulations. It was, however, more successful in freeing up trade within Europe, and in giving a greater role to the private sector in the recovery and re-building processes (Wood 1986; Kunz 1997; Esposito 1994; Grant and Nijman 1997).

In the early 1950s, despite the promise of Truman's Point Four Program, a skeptical Congress and a more national security–conscious Eisenhower administration made cuts in foreign aid in favor of increased military spending, and it was to be nearly another decade before US and Western foreign aid increased and became more sharply defined, with a development objective rather than a security objective (Hagen and Ruttan 1988; Parker 2006; Picard and Buss 2009).

During the first half of the 1950s, Asia experienced what Parker (2006, 872) called a "…seemingly endless crisis in the region [and further afield], as from north to south along the East Asian coast, fighting waxed and waned." The idea of using foreign aid as a soft power tool to contain communism did not appeal to the US administration in the same way as the British Commonwealth–led Colombo Plan. The Colombo Plan[3] was a mix of technical support and training, and probably the first example of South-South cooperation. Likewise, Japan was using its reparation payments to countries it had occupied during World War II for broader development objectives as well as for containing communism. Hara Yasusaburo, then president of the Nippon Kayaku Corporation, observed:

> …we can contribute to the economic development of South-east Asia in the name of reparation payments; we can help prevent the propagation of communism. With reparations, we can kill two birds with one stone. (quoted in Suehiro, 1999, 88).

The US approach to foreign aid and development in the Global South in the 1950s was largely hands-off: "…the Eisenhower team's basic approach to the Third World: a focus on covert and/or psychological operations, hints at economic aid, the use of pro-American proxies, and where possible a light touch" (Parker 2006, 883). This approach was also due to the Congress being fearful of a possible Marshall Plan to the Global South on a grand scale, and concern at the high cost of the Korean War. US aid at that time was very much on a modest scale, and went hand in hand with military assistance (United States Congress 1957a; Tansky 1967). US General Alfred Gruenther noted in 1952 that "…the economic and military aspects of defense…defy separation [in modern warfare]" (quoted in Hagen and Ruttan 1988, 3). Foreign aid was used to "…support a system of interlocking anti-communist alliances beginning with NATO" (Morley and Morley 1961, 9).

The only development aspect to the US aid program was to "… afford friendly leaders an opportunity to maintain their authority and legitimacy by delivering better services to their citizens" (Picard and Buss 2009, 87). The intended outcome of the program was greater political stability rather than economic growth, and any activities had to be argued on grounds of the American military interest rather than developmental need (US Congress 1957, 13). The proportion of military aid to development aid rose from 24 percent in 1951 to 66 percent in 1953, after Eisenhower took office (p. 8). The clear exceptions to this were the Colombo Plan, mentioned above, to which the US contribution was modest, and food aid.[4]

> *The intended outcome of the US aid program was greater political stability rather than economic growth*

By the mid-1950s, the United States was facing the Soviet Union as a direct competitor in using foreign aid as soft power and, as Secretary of State Dulles noted, "…with more guile and less force" (Hagen and Ruttan 1988, 5), while at the same time an economic downturn in the US limited budgetary options. Eisenhower was concerned with the rise of Soviet economic aid to developing countries but was unsure as to how to respond: "US policymakers took the Soviet challenge to heart but were very uncertain of where else to take it" (*ibid.*). Despite the clear pressure on US strategic interests, Congress remained reluctant to give Eisenhower the foreign aid funding he required and so he had to look further afield.

Eisenhower approached other Western donors and allies, such as Japan, to pick up the slack. As a result, Western aid doubled in the five years 1956–1960 from what it was over the previous five years

Patrick Kilby

(Morrison 1998; Jain 2016; Griffin 1991). The Eisenhower administration then launched a Western partnership for development cooperation, the Common Aid Effort, to cement Western support for foreign aid (Scott 2015), and put pressure on other Western donors to support the US anti-Soviet effort (White 1974). The idea was to burden-share among Western allies to increase the volume of Western development aid in the face of what was seen as a Soviet aid onslaught (Verschaeve and Orbie 2015a; Westad 2005; Tansky 1967).[5]

The Soviet foreign aid effort started after Stalin's death in 1953 and grew quickly, marking a brief period of soft power rivalry with the United States (Goldman 1967; Tansky 1967; Lancaster 2008). While Soviet aid outside the communist bloc did not match US aid in volume, its strategic use led to the perception that Soviet aid was both substantial and effective (Hattori 2001; Orr 1988; Goldman 1967). Inside the Soviet bloc, the aid effort was considerable, with large volumes of Soviet aid to support China's industrialization in the 1950s, which Westad refers to as the Soviet "Marshall Plan to modernize China" (2005, 69).

Flagship projects, which the United States and the World Bank declined to fund, such as the Aswan High Dam in Egypt, gave the Soviet Union propaganda wins and developing countries a clear choice as well as the ability to bargain the terms of Western aid (White 1974; Wood 1986). Soviet aid was in the form of loans at half the interest rate of US aid, and because repayments were not required to be made in a convertible currency, barter arrangements were common. In some cases, according to Goldman (1967), US aid was recycled to the Soviets: the loan repayments were made with US PL 480 food aid, which the Soviet Union then sold on the world market, keeping the foreign exchange (Goldman 1967, 72). Soviet Premier Nikita Khrushchev even made the point that without Soviet aid there would be much less Western aid, and so the Soviet Union should get some of the credit for that (Tansky 1967; Wood 1986).

The United States was also hampered in its soft power diplomacy by the perception within developing countries that the US government policy to its own people of color was fundamentally racist. The US racial segregation battles of the 1950s gave the impression to developing countries that the US aid program was influenced by what was seen as racially-based values, which the Soviet Union, and later

China, played up in their propaganda efforts to the Global South (Jones 2005; Angelo and Davies 2015; Westad 2005; Abraham 2008; Parker 2006; Jones 2005; Brazinksy 2017).

In 1961, the logjam in the US Congress on foreign aid was broken, in part due to the importance the new president, John F. Kennedy, placed on it, and in part to the persuasive skills he brought to the table (Hagen and Ruttan 1988). The Kennedy administration went beyond the idea of burden sharing and called for a renewed push for more foreign aid, by calling for a UN-led Decade for Development (Kennedy 1961). Kennedy also introduced a new approach to international development in the form of the Partners for Progress program, to offer a positive alternative to the Soviet Union's aid program (Kennedy 1962; Hagen and Ruttan 1988). It was a marked shift from the 1950s philosophy of the Mutual Security Act which stipulated "…that aid could only be extended to strengthen the free world" and complement military aid (Orr 1988, 741). The US aid program was consolidated into a new agency, AID, and the Peace Corps program was started as an extension of soft power (Hagen and Ruttan 1988; Labouisse 1961). The aim of AID in the early 1960s was "linking the twin ideological foundations of capitalist economic growth and political resistance to international communism" (Essex 2008, 234). This harked directly back to the Truman Point Four Program and the separation of development aid from military aid. Foreign aid was to be used in support of market-based capitalism, and in Kennedy's case, to include the promotion of US exports and investment in Africa (Angelo and Davies 2015).

While the Kennedy program represented a permanent shift in US aid policy to focus on longer-term development, with grants rather than loans for programs and over longer periods, the commitment to increased funding was short-lived. As the Soviet Union reduced its aid program, so did the US, so that by 1968 the budget outlay for foreign aid was half of what it was in 1962 (Shapiro and Weiner 2002; Fleck and Kilby 2010). There were even questions in Congress of the need for an aid program at all when the US economy was stagnating (Fleck and Kilby 2010; Essex 2008; DAC Secretariat 1970; Picard and Buss 2009). Interestingly, the rapid increase in the Chinese aid program in the 1970s did not prompt a commensurate increase in the US aid program (Fleck and Kilby 2010); the US-China détente of 1972 may have played a part in this decoupling. In the 2000s, the Bush administration's policy shift to a security focus in foreign aid harked back to the Eisenhower administration policies with the increase in the aid program to fund the War on Terror (Howell and Lind 2009; Moss, Standley, and Roodman 2005).

Since the 1970s the US aid program has followed a similar philosophy: while it was a projection of US power, it was also a projection of US liberal values and its manifest destiny in pursuing them. Later, at the end of the Cold War, democratization in recipient countries was added to the list of liberal values being promoted (Zoysa 2005; Picard and Buss 2009). During the Cold War, it made political sense for the United States to support authoritarian regimes as they were more reliable partners, and certainly seen as preferable to left-wing or even left-leaning democracies such as India or Chile in the early 1970s (Hook and Rumsey 2016; Liska 1961).

While Soviet Union funding of foreign aid fell sharply in the 1960s, and the US program followed suit, the Chinese aid program increased and offered a quite different strategy to the US policy of Cold War containment of communism and the promotion of US values. While Mao Zedong spoke of exporting revolution, first Premier Zhou Enlai was embarking on a diplomatic campaign across the South to build Southern solidarity to challenge both US and Soviet hegemony (Samy 2010; Larkin 1973; Huisken 2013; Brazinsky 2017). Key to Zhou's approach were the ideas of partnership and solidarity, which are enshrined in the Five Principles of Peaceful Coexistence (1954) and the Eight Principles of Foreign Aid (1964) (Gill and Huang 2006; Varrall 2016; Mawdsley 2012). In keeping with these principles China has consistently challenged the Western liberal views of democracy and human rights (Mawdsley, Savage, and Kim 2014). Zhou used the Geneva Peace Conference of 1954 and the Bandung Conference of 1955 to position China as a leader in building solidarity across the South, with foreign aid playing a central part of that process (Brazinsky 2017). In the 2000s this solidarity was strengthened with closer economic cooperation and higher levels of Chinese aid as well as foreign direct investment both from state and private sources, at first in Africa and then extending to West, Central, and South Asia in the 2010s with the Belt Road Initiative.

Bandung and the Origin of Chinese Foreign Aid Programs

China's foreign aid program had its origins in the dissatisfaction with what the Global South saw as Western hegemony in the postcolonial development processes. The Bandung Conference and ideas of South-South cooperation had their origins in a series of meetings from the turn of the twentieth century. Prior to the decolonization of the late 1940s into the 1960s, the emerging developing country leaders had been active in trying to have their voices heard in global forums, beginning

> *China's program had its origins in dissatisfaction with what the Global South saw as Western hegemony*

around 1900. This included the first Pan-African Conference held in London in 1900 (Hongoh 2016), a peace conference in 1926 held at Bierville near Paris that declared that "Asia must have a rightful place in the consideration of world problems" (Birchall 2016; Appadorai 1955, 1), and the Brussels anti-imperial conference of 1927 where the Indian independence leader Jawaharlal Nehru took a leading role (Abraham 2014; Hongoh 2016; Acharya 2016).

These conferences followed what was seen as a snub at the Paris Peace Conference of 1919 to the nationalist and regional aspirations of Japan, China, and others in the refusal to include an anti–racial discrimination clause in the Treaty of Versailles, or to give back the former German concession territory of Shandong to China (Kawamura 1997; Hongoh 2016; Brazinsky 2017).[6] Given the role to that date of the "white" colonial powers in international relations and development, the Indonesian President Sukarno noted in his opening address at Bandung that it was "…the first international conference of coloured peoples in the history of mankind," and the idea of oppressed peoples dominated it (Jones 2005, 861; Parker 2006; Wright 1956; Ampiah 2007; Hongoh 2016).

The post–World War II independence processes also built momentum for a Southern voice in global affairs. After the war, there were a series of meetings of Asian and African leaders dealing with issues of decolonization, leading up to Bandung. The Pan-African

Conference of future African leaders in Manchester in 1945 (Cheru 2016) was followed by the Asian Relations Conference held in Delhi in 1947. The Delhi conference challenged the notion of Western civilization as the zenith, arguing in favor of the strength and enduring history of Eastern civilizations, and put forward the idea of Arab-Asian regional cooperation (Abraham 2008; Vieira 2016). One outcome of the Delhi conference was the idea that "'Asian knowledge' would be offered to the world without conditions" (Abraham 2008, 201). The Baguio Conference in the Philippines followed in 1950 and went a step further and articulated Nehru's brand of neutralism, which he brought to Bandung and then to the nonaligned movement (Ampiah 2007; Appadorai 1955). The Geneva Peace Conference of 1954, where the peace settlements for the Korean War and the Indochina conflict were thrashed out, established China and Zhou Enlai in particular as important interlocutors on the world stage (Brazinsky 2017). This reputation was in evidence at Bandung and set in train China's rise as a leader of the Global South.

In April 1954 five South Asian leaders[7] met in Colombo and declared that "colonialism was a violation of fundamental human rights and a threat to world peace," and set in train a process for a much wider global conference than any that hitherto had been held (Jones 2005, 852). The Colombo declaration was also in part a response to the US moves to establish the South East Asian Treaty Organization (SEATO) as a bulwark against communism. SEATO had the problem of being dominated by Western (white) powers, with Thailand and the Philippines as the only regional treaty partners (Parker 2006; Jones 2005). As a result there was a strong anti-Western racial undercurrent in the Colombo discussions despite most of the leaders present being trenchantly anti-communist. Questions were raised as to whether "white" countries in the region (i.e., Australia and New Zealand) that had been observers at some of the planning meetings should be invited (Wright 1956; Parker 2006; Jones 2005; Ampiah 2007). The West, likewise, wanted no part in the conference. Acharya (2016, 343) quoted declassified cables about Australia's involvement:

He [Prime Minister Menzies] takes a dark view of activities which, under guise of peaceful co-existence, in fact are stirring up colour prejudices (from a UK High Commission note in early 1955). Another British document points out that the Australian government 'neither wanted an invitation nor the opportunity to refuse one.'

Similarly, the United States did not want to send observers and kept an official distance, but could not prevent an African-American congressman from attending (Parker 2006). The call for a clearer voice from the South was led by Nehru and his passionate objections to SEATO, to counter what they saw as Western hegemony (Acharya 2016; Fisher 1971). The heart of these objections was less about containing communism than about US exceptionalism or its manifest destiny (Zoysa 2005; Picard and Buss 2009). These were ideas used by Jefferson in his intervention against pirates on the west coast of Africa in the early nineteenth century: "the aim was both to secure US commerce and impose American standards of behavior" (Westad 2005, 21). To outsiders, SEATO also seemed to echo Rudyard Kipling's racially-based notion of the "white man's burden" (Kipling and Balestier 1899).[8] The Bandung Conference was held, in part, to challenge both the notion of the United States' manifest destiny and the "white man's burden" (Parker 2006).

The great achievement of that week at Bandung was to bring together political leaders from erstwhile adversaries in different political camps to seek common ground. "The image of the torch of civilizations being passed to new continents outside Europe was omnipresent among the Third World leaders at Bandung" (Westad 2005, 99). Western allies, Soviet allies, and the nonaligned were represented, agreeing to put their differences aside to reach a consensus (there were no votes) and a single voice: "...endowed with metaphorical power [and] indignation...against the injustices of the international political system as designed at Yalta" (Ampiah 2007, 2). There were 29 attendees:[9] those representing the three main Western alliances (NATO, CENTO,[10] and SEATO) and US bilateral allies and supporters such as Japan, Ceylon, and South Vietnam; Soviet allies and supporters such as China and North Vietnam; and a number who were variously nonaligned. The key outcome of Bandung, after a long, bitter debate about whether the Soviet Union was a colonial power in Eastern Europe, was a clear statement against colonialism "...in all its forms"[11] (Acharya 2016; Parker 2006).

The Bandung Conference represented the crossroads of several key Cold War trends: the old specter of communism and the newer one of neutralism; the vectors of anti-colonialism and Third World nationalism; and a stirring consciousness of changes in inter- and intranational race relations (Parker 2006, 888).

There was an attempt to have a follow-up conference to Bandung, which would be more inclusive, with the idea being put forward by China and Indonesia in the early 1960s. There was a preparatory meeting in Indonesia in 1964 with the main meeting to occur in Algiers in 1965. India was ambivalent about the conference as the ongoing tensions it had with Pakistan and China had worsened. In what was regarded as a spoiling move, India wanted the Soviet Union to attend, which India knew China would not countenance. At the very last minute the meeting was deferred and then later cancelled, due to the politics of the Sino-Soviet split, India's ambivalence, and objections to China's wish to set a radical agenda for the conference (Abraham 2008; Berger 2004; Brazinsky 2017). There was a 50th anniversary conference in 2005, held in Bandung and Jakarta with 106 countries from Asia

> *The key outcome of Bandung was a clear statement against colonialism '…in all its forms'*

and Africa attending. The outcomes of the 50th anniversary conference are enshrined in the New Asian-African Strategic Partnership (NAASP), which recommitted to the principles of Bandung and expanded them into clearer statements based on three Bandung pillars: political solidarity; economic cooperation; and sociocultural relations (Assie-Lumumba 2015).

Bandung's enduring legacy was to lay the groundwork for the nonaligned movement. "[Bandung]…constituted the first major collective assertion by a group of developing countries of the doctrine of nonalignment" (White 1974, 204; Parker 2006; Assie-Lumumba 2015). This is probably an overstatement as more than half of the attendees were in either the Soviet or the US camp at the time, and the conference carefully avoided references to the Cold War, a central plank of the nonaligned movement (Abraham 2008). While Nkrumah and Tito,[12] who were part of the leadership of the nonaligned movement, did not attend the conference (for different reasons), they were very much influenced by the meeting:

> Bandung became the touchstone of a wide array of initiatives associated directly and indirectly with Third Worldism. The idea of the Third World was increasingly deployed to generate unity and support among a growing number of non-aligned nation-states whose leaders sought to displace the 'East–West' (Cold War) conflict and foreground the 'North–South' conflict (Berger 2004, 10).

The first point of the Bandung Conference declaration articulated the need for mutual cooperation, both economic and cultural, between and within Asia and Africa, and the declaration agreed "…to provide technical assistance to one another" (Republic of Indonesia 1955, 1). The basis of the declaration was in the idea of developing countries supporting each other, rather than depending on what were seen as colonial or neocolonial "masters." What was to become known as South-South cooperation was to grow and be influential over the following decades (Appadorai 1955; Wright 1956; Mawdsley 2012), so that by the 2010s new institutions such as the BRICS[13], Asian Infrastructure Investment Bank (AIIB), and Belt Road Initiative (BRI) openly challenged the influence of the International Monetary Fund (IMF), World Bank, and the Development Assistance Committee (DAC) of the OECD.

As the noted African-American writer Richard Wright rather presciently noted in his report on the conference, the clause on economic cooperation sounded innocent enough but that:

> …the "Yellow Peril" as Jack London[14] conceived it was not primarily a racial matter it was economic. When the day comes that Asian and African raw materials are processed in Asia and Africa by labor whose needs are not as inflated as those of the western laborers the supremacy of the western world economic cultural and political will have been broken once and for all (Wright 1956, 203).

The basic philosophy of South-South cooperation envisaged at the time, and continuing into the 21st century, is that of reciprocity, shared values, and solidarity, which challenges the "hierarchical mindset" of Western aid (Mawdsley 2012, 257). As Yeh and Wharton argue, while the DAC is "…couching true Overseas Development Assistance (ODA) in terms of altruism by one party; the Chinese Government's approach, neither seeks nor values such a distinction" (Yeh and Wharton 2016, 293). South-South cooperation is about developing social bonds through the mutuality of "gift giving" rather than one-way grants that are based on charity, with the associated notions of paternalism and dependency. Hattori (2001, 635) refers to this as "symbolic domination," and it continues to dog Southern perceptions of Western aid (Mawdsley 2012; Hynes and Scott 2013; Yeh and Wharton 2016). In practice, however, the two approaches have more in common than these distinctions suggest. The practical differences lie in the longer-term nature and mutuality of the South-South relationship, thus fewer political, economic, or structural conditions are imposed but as Mattlin and Nojonen (2015, 720) argue, the process of conditionality is more complex:

> …extensive reliance on funding for critical infrastructure from one source country can conceivably result in structural dependency that over time may also create political dependency. However, the conditionalities that we have identified are not imposed by the Chinese state as explicit policy conditions that require changes to national economic policies.

Either because it felt threatened or due to ignorance, the West tended to ignore both the Third World and the Eastern bloc as players in those early aid debates. Bartsh of the DAC, for example, was:

> …astonished by the fact that neither the state department or the UN nor private researchers paid any attention to the relatively considerable aid effort of the communist donor countries in favour of communist less developed countries, Only aid to non-communist less developed countries were counted and compared to western aid efforts (Bartsch 1969a, 1).

After Bandung the Chinese aid program had a major shift in focus so that in addition to supporting its communist neighbors and ideological partners, it also moved to support a much broader group of countries where it competed directly with Soviet and Western aid, while at the same time being a major recipient of large amounts of Soviet aid (Westad 2005).[15] The only condition imposed for receiving China's aid was support for the One China Policy and the consequent breaking of any formal ties the recipient might have with Taiwan (DAC Secretariat 1978; Samy 2010; Campbell 2016; Sautman and Yan 2007).[16] This condition has both softened in the 2000s, and hardened again in the 2010s, as a response to the strength of sentiment for independence by the relevant Taiwanese government.

China Emerges as a Donor

Chinese Premier Zhou Enlai used Bandung to mark China's entry onto the world stage. While Mao Zedong captured the headlines with revolutionary rhetoric and his support for revolutionary movements, Zhou was a seasoned diplomat and brought a message of a more moderate Chinese foreign policy (Jian 2008; Brazinsky 2017). The Five Principles of Peaceful Coexistence, which Zhou introduced in 1954 at the India-China peace negotiations in New Delhi, were emphasized at Bandung: "mutual respect for sovereignty and territorial integrity; mutual non-aggression; non-interference in each other's internal affairs; equality and mutual benefit; and peaceful coexistence" (Varrall 2016, 24; Mattlin and Nojonen 2015; Narayanan 2004). Zhou's language at Bandung eschewed communist rhetoric, and was very much in solidarity with other developing countries. As Wright (1956, 159) noted, Zhou knew: "...he was addressing lonely men whose mentalities had been branded with a sense of being outcasts. It cost him nothing to make such a gesture," and Wright goes on to observe that Zhou was the first communist to acknowledge that "... he and his fellow Chinese were suffering, were backward, were afraid of war" (p. 164). With this quite understated performance Zhou won over many of his critics, making the unyielding United States "... appear churlish and intransigent" (Ampiah 2007, 44). The United States struggled to respond to Zhou and Bandung, and ultimately it was a missed opportunity:

Bandung helped to prompt the American conclusion that European colonialism was becoming more a Western liability than an asset. But the abstract conclusion did not produce concrete action (Parker 2006, 888).

The exception may have been the US abandonment of the British and French in the Suez crisis, which marked the end of the already declining British Empire (Acharya 2016; Kyle 1991; Brazinsky 2017). Zhou used his personal relationships to smooth over border tensions with Burma and disputes over islands around Taiwan, and set in train South-South dialogue (Appadorai 1955; Jones 2005; Brazinsky 2017). It was at the conference that Zhou built personal ties with Nasser of Egypt, which led to a Chinese trade office being established in Cairo 1956, and substantial military and other support just short of troops being provided in the Suez crisis. In return China purchased Egyptian cotton, and a training program for Egyptians was set up in China (Larkin 1973; OECD-DAC 1979; Cheng 2010; Brazinsky 2017). This nascent program in Africa expanded to Yemen in 1958, Guinea in 1959, and Ghana and Mali in the early 1960s, as well as supporting the Asia-Africa solidarity fund (DAC Secretariat 1964; Larkin 1973). Technical assistance, which started in Algeria in 1963, led to mobile medical teams being sent to developing countries on a two-year rotation, treating around 50,000 patients per year. In addition, some 700 African students went to Chinese universities in the 1960s prior to the Cultural Revolution (OECD-DAC 1979)[17].

> *By the mid-1960s, Chinese aid was evenly distributed between South and Southeast Asia and Africa*

By the mid-1960s, Chinese aid was evenly distributed between South and Southeast Asia and Africa, with Pakistan, Egypt, and Indonesia as the main recipients. In Asia, China provided aid to Cambodia and Indonesia in 1956, Nepal and Sri Lanka in 1957, and Burma in 1959. All in all, programs were started in 20 countries in Asia and Africa post-Bandung (Cheng 2010). The growth in Chinese aid in the 1960s and 1970s was related to China's 1962 rift with the Soviet Union. It allowed China to compete with both the Soviet Union and the United States for political influence in the South, offering an alternative to the Cold War adversaries, with the aim to position itself as leader of the Global South (Westad 2005; Berger 2004; Shen and Li 2015; Brazinsky 2017).

The rift with the Soviet Union has been explained as ideological, around the direction of China's economic development and the pace of the Great Leap Forward (Westad 2005; Berger 2004; Fisher 1971; Shen and Li 2015; Jersild 2014). It is also possible that it had its origins in the repayments being made to the Soviets, at the same time as the famine, for their large aid program to China through the 1950s, which may have been seen as a way of tying China to the Soviet Union as a vassal state (Ashton et al. 1994; Chang and Halliday 2007; Westad 2005; Fisher 1971; Xue 2014). Given China's history of "100 years of humiliation" at the hands of imperialist powers, the causes of the rift ran deep (Taylor 1998; Henderson 2008).

The rift with the Soviet Union led China to use foreign aid to shift developing countries away from the Soviet orbit (Westad 2005; Hoeffding 1963; Larkin 1973). The United States was also worried about Chinese expansion and responded with a strong diplomatic campaign against China across the continent, but the newly installed Johnson administration differed markedly from Kennedy on foreign aid, and failed to match its diplomatic campaign with a comprehensive aid program (Brazinsky 2017; DeRoche 2007). In late 1963, early 1964, Zhou Enlai visited ten African countries with a large delegation of senior officials to negotiate aid and trade deals. Out of this visit came China's Eight Principles of Foreign Aid[18] that built on the Five Principles of Peaceful Coexistence (Enlai 1964; DAC Secretariat 1978; Cheng 2010; Shinn and Eisenman 2012; Varrall 2016; Larkin 1973). These Eight Principles have been the bedrock of Chinese foreign aid over the past 50 years and are often reiterated to contrast China's approach to Western foreign aid policies (Cheng 2010; Varrall 2016; Xue 2014; Niu 2016). The visit also set up the nascent trade links with Africa that expanded rapidly in the 2000s (Besada and O'Bright 2017; Cheng 2016).

From Zhou's Africa visit came the rapid expansion in Chinese foreign aid to the continent, and in 1972 China's aid peaked at $450m due in part to the expenditure on the iconic TAZARA railway which foreshadowed China's massive rail investment in Africa and Asia in the

2010s (OECD-DAC 1979; Maurice 1975; Anthony 2013; Huang and Chen 2016). While China generally eschewed supporting large infrastructure projects, the railway linking Zambian copper mines to ports in Tanzania was the clear exception (Bartsch 1969b; Larkin 1973; Monson 2006; Song 2015). Zambia had initially approached the British and the Americans to fund the railway, which it needed for its copper exports to bypass white-ruled Rhodesia and South Africa and their threat of blockade. When US President Johnson bluntly declined Zambia's request, President Kaunda had no choice but to go to China (which already had a partnership with socialist Tanzania), even though he was anti-communist and very suspicious of China's intentions in Africa (DeRoche 2007; Song 2015; Brazinsky 2017). China's aid diplomacy with Zambia and socialist Tanzania was used to outflank both the Soviet Union and the West.

At nearly 2,000 km in length, the TAZARA railway was and still is China's largest single aid project, and involved 14,000 Chinese and 38,000 African workers in its construction (Monson 2013, 2006; Song 2015). The railway was started in 1970 and was completed in 1975, a year ahead of schedule (Larkin 1973; DAC Secretariat 1978; Song 2015). It made an unambiguous statement about Chinese technical capacity and its political solidarity with the newly independent nations of Africa (Brazinsky 2017). It was a direct challenge to apartheid South Africa's "colonial" control of its neighbors in Southern Africa, and the tacit support South Africa was being provided from the West in general, and the United States in particular (Berger 2004; DeRoche 2007; Angelo and Davies 2015). In the 2010s China returned to railway construction in East Africa, with new lines linking the port of Mombasa with Nairobi then on to Uganda and Rwanda, as well as lines further afield in Nigeria, Ethiopia, Sudan, and Angola (Huang and Chen 2016; Anthony 2013).

By the mid-1970s Pakistan, Tanzania, and Zambia were the largest recipients (outside the socialist bloc) of Chinese aid (DAC Secretariat 1978). While the aid was tied to the use of Chinese goods and services for much of the work, loans were granted at times in a convertible currency, and were often repaid with exports of commodities to China in a barter arrangement, and at highly concessional rates. China also commonly rescheduled debts or converted loans to grants. Their philosophy, in line with the Eight Principles, was to use intermediate technology and labor-intensive methods, with Chinese personnel being paid at local rates. As these labor costs were less than half that of other donors, the DAC argued that the aid was:

> ...certainly worth more than the nominal loan amounts and perhaps 35% could be added to the face value of loan agreements...China's aid and advice are seen by many developing countries as valuable because China itself is facing many of their problems (DAC Secretariat 1978, 4).

The grant element of Chinese aid in the 1970s was very high, at 75–85 percent, much higher than Western aid (DAC Secretariat 1978), and while no value was placed on the technical services, they were estimated at around one billion dollars over the 20 years from 1955 to 1975 (p. 19). Measuring China's aid using DAC definitions in order to make comparisons is vexed both then and now. Simple comparisons cannot be made without generally making gross underestimates of the value of China's foreign aid, due to a lack of access to reliable and comparable data; definitional issues around the extent to which subsidized loans, trade credits, and debt cancellations are counted; and how technical assistance is valued (Bräutigam 2011b; Dreher et al. 2016; Hook and Rumsey 2016; Kitano 2014).[19]

In the 1970s, towards the end of the Cultural Revolution, China's aid program grew rapidly as a result of Zhou's outward-looking foreign policy, leading to greater global engagement. Two-thirds of China's total cumulative commitments from the 1950s to the 1970s (over $4.3b) were made between 1970 and 1977. By 1977 Chinese aid was reaching over 70 countries. Like most aid programs at the time, there were complaints

In the 1970s, China's aid program grew rapidly as a result of Zhou's outward-looking foreign policy

of slow progress, poor-quality equipment, and a general lack of spare parts (DAC Secretariat 1978, 9). Three-quarters of China's aid in the 1970s was bilateral project assistance, including providing Chinese consumer goods to be sold to cover local costs.[20] The typical Chinese aid project in Africa (apart from the TAZARA railway) was a pilot farm or a small-scale light industrial plant with import substitution as a main driver, while in Asia it was roads and power plants built by Chinese workers (DAC Secretariat 1978).

China and the Nonaligned Movement

While China did not formally join the nonaligned movement until 2000, when the first South Summit of the Group of 77 (G77) and China was held in Havana, China was very close to the nonaligned movement, and the related G77 group at the UN, from its inception in the mid-1960s (Solíz 2014; Brazinsky 2017). A key point made at the first nonaligned movement meetings in the early 1960s was that the more dangerous division was between the haves and the have-nots, rather than between the East and West; and as a result the G77 argued for a more just global economic system (Nesadurai 2008). While the nonaligned movement was less concerned with foreign aid, it was instrumental in the establishment of the United Nations Conference on Trade and Development (UNCTAD), which did have a direct focus on foreign aid and development. The G77 developing-country bloc in the UN provided the nonaligned movement a united voice in UN debates (Nesadurai 2008; Abraham 2008; Berger 2004). For a time, UNCTAD was a rival to the DAC, reflecting developing-country voices and aspirations (Berger 2004; Jolly et al. 2004; Carroll and Hynes 2013). It lobbied for large increases in foreign aid and attacked donor attitudes (DAC Secretariat 1973; 1972; 1965; Clemens and Moss 2007; Hynes and Scott 2013; Crane 1984), all at a time when foreign aid from China and OPEC was rapidly increasing. For example, in 1978 OPEC accounted for one-third of all foreign aid (Mawdsley 2012). These debates serve to highlight that South-South cooperation, for example with OPEC and China, was a viable alternative to the West and the Soviet Union.

> *The more dangerous division was between the haves and the have-nots, rather than between the East and West*

UNCTAD supported a more Keynesian approach to national government policy, and challenged the free market ideology that the West and the international trade system led by the OECD and DAC were increasingly pushing. UNCTAD argued that these systems discriminated against state-owned enterprises and state-led interventions, and focused on narrow financial returns of aid projects rather than their broader economic impacts (Dell 1984; Nesadurai 2008; Lavelle 2013; Koehler 2015). Robert McNamara, as the recently installed head of the World Bank, was well aware of these challenges and in a speech at Colombia University in early 1970 said:

> But when the distribution of land, income and opportunity becomes distorted to the point of desperation, what political leaders must often weigh is the risk of unpopular but necessary social reform against the risk of social rebellion. 'Too little too late' is history's most universal epitaph for political regimes which have lost their mandate to the demands of landless, jobless, disenfranchised and desperate men (quoted in Maddux 1981, 15).

But these exhortations by McNamara had little effect, either within the Bank or among Western donors. As Miles noted a few years earlier on the prospect of UNCTAD: "…the division between rich and poor is the division between those with the power to take decisions in the economic sphere and those who have to accept them" (1968, 71). While the idea and rhetoric of prioritizing aid for basic human needs was strong at the time, development practice itself told a different story. For example, the focus on agriculture and the green revolution, which was ostensibly about reaching the poor and marginal farmers, actually led to support for larger, more capital-intensive agriculture, and the poor remained marginalized (DAC Secretariat 1973; Griffin 1991; Evenson and Gollin 2003; Patel 2013).

In the 1970s the G77 took a step further with the passing of a UN resolution calling for a New International Economic Order (NIEO), which China enthusiastically supported (Cheng and Shi 2009). This "…flowed from, and built on, earlier efforts to address the structural inequalities of the international political-economic order" (Berger 2004, 23). It was a Keynesian response to the issues at the time (Nesadurai 2008). Given the failure of the first Development Decade, declining terms of trade for developing countries, falling levels of real aid, a global financial crisis, and the global oil crises, developing countries argued that the Bretton Woods institutions and related global systems were in dire need of reform. The success of OPEC in using the price of oil as a weapon against a hegemonic West gave the movement something of a (albeit short-term) fillip (Clark 1977; Woods 2008; Carroll and Hynes 2013; Jolly et al. 2004).[21] The Brandt Commission that reviewed foreign aid and development in the late 1970s picked up many of the ideas of the G77 and NIEO, and called for new arrangements to meet the central objective of a transfer of greater power to the South under the central theme of "mutuality of interests" (ODI 1980, 1; Brandt Commission 1979). This was in line with Zhou's Eight Principles and some reappeared, in rhetoric at least, in the DAC Paris Principles of Foreign Aid some 20 years later (Verschaeve and Orbie 2015b).

While the NIEO was a very powerful idea of the 1970s, it was destined to be short-lived and replaced by the US-led globalization project of the 1980s (Berger 2004). This globalization project represented a move away "…from international Keynesianism and the search for international economic justice" (Nesadurai 2008, 84). The 1980s debt crisis and the Reagan and Thatcher radical neoliberal economic policies and their influence in the World Bank became the new norm, leading to what became known as the lost decade in terms of economic development (Carrasco 1999; Drabek and Laird 1998; Morgan 2001).

> …it is the height of irony that the most radical appeal for national sovereignty and control over economic activities in the post war period should be followed by the greatest surrender of control over national policies in the 1980s (Jolly et al. 2004, 123).

It can be argued that the shift to a Keynesian focus on filling infrastructure gaps taken by China and other Southern donors in the 2000s is a return to the themes of the NIEO. The 1980s was also a period when China was going through its own internal reforms and seeking large sums of foreign aid from the World Bank and Japan to finance its path to rapid economic growth. This, coupled with Deng Xiaoping's reluctance to send any more foreign aid to Africa or elsewhere, further added to the woes of the lost decade (Besada and O'Bright 2017).

The reemergence of China as a donor in the 1990s and its positive response to its neighbors' plight during the Asian Economic Crisis (Huisken 2013; Acharya 1999; Higgott 1998) marked another step in China's path to leadership of other powerful southern states in the 2000s. This has enabled a global alliance of South-South cooperation (the BRICS), as well as the G77 plus China, to challenge the West and its set of neoliberal norms and conditions that still drives its aid philosophy. This challenge was not possible in the 1970s with the NIEO. This shift represented a more Keynesian-inspired statist approach to development explained by New Structural Economics (Solíz 2014; Suehiro 1999; Koehler 2015; Yeung 2017; Lin 2011; Wang, Ozanne, and Hao 2014). Part of this is the development of quite a different set of multilateral institutions, including the Asian Infrastructure Investment Bank (AIIB), the New Development (BRICS) Bank, and the Silk Road Fund (Ban and Blyth 2013; Strand, Flores, and Trevathan 2016).

In the 1980s the growth in Chinese aid slowed as China focused on its own rapid development, and as it discovered that it was competing with Africa for the World Bank loans it felt it was eligible for due to its need, capacity, and low income levels. This was to be an ongoing issue through the 1980s as the United States cut its IDA contributions and the scale of China's need dwarfed that of Africa (World Bank 1985, 1983, 1982a, b). In contrast to Zhao, the new Chinese leader Deng Xiaoping felt that African countries were less important in China's modernization process, and this led to nearly a decade of "outright neglect" (Besada and O'Bright 2017, 656). During a 1982 visit to 11 African countries, Premier Zhao Ziyang announced that China would move to a "…more mutually beneficial engagement" (Yeh and Wharton 2016, 292), following Deng's exhortation of "…giving moderately and receiving a lot" (quoted in Jerve 2007, 3). The upshot was that the competition with the Soviet Union and the United States was over, and Africa should be less dependent on Chinese aid unless it was driven by mutual economic partnerships (Cheng and Shi 2009). In 1985 China went a step further and criticized Africa and the developing world more generally for "errors in policy-making" (Taylor 1998, 445).

This policy of aid to Africa being based on mutual economic benefit gave way in the 1990s to it being based on mixed strategic and economic benefits, after the crackdown in 1989 following the Tiananmen Square protests threatened to again isolate China from the global stage (Huisken 2013; Besada and O'Bright 2017). Deng appreciated that many countries in Africa had only given muted criticism of the Chinese government actions, if not tacit support, and China responded accordingly (Taylor 1998; Huisken 2013; Samy 2010). Chinese Foreign Minister Qian Qichen visited 14 African capitals after the crackdown, and aid to the continent was boosted dramatically (Cheng and Shi 2009).

After a decade of little change, China's aid to Africa increased from $300m in 1987 to $1.8b in 2002 (Samy 2010). In addition, after China became a net importer of energy in 1995, a new set of linkages to the resource-rich countries of Africa was established. This led to a rapid increase in Chinese state and private investment to parallel the aid program, from $51.19m between 1979 and 1990, to $2.1b in 2010 alone (Besada and O'Bright 2017, 657). This burgeoning relationship with Africa was institutionalized in 2000 with the Forum on China Africa Cooperation (FOCAC), which has since become the avenue for reaching broad agreements and signaling levels of commitment. In the 2000s, the Africa program is more strategic, with a focus on mutual benefit and Africa's increased economic growth, thereby providing a market for China's output. FOCAC soon expanded its horizons and by the third ministerial meeting in Beijing it was working towards:

> *China's aid to Africa increased from $300m in 1987 to $1.8b in 2002*

...the establishment of a new international political and economic order that is fair and just in the twenty-first century; and how to promote Sino-African economic and trade co-operation (Cheng and Shi 2009, 92).

The Chinese foreign aid program has been part of China's ongoing process of establishing itself in the world, not only in solidarity with its southern partners, but also on the global stage, where the aid program has acted as a symbol of soft power to establish Chinese credibility and leadership (Gill and Huang 2006). China's focus was mainly on project aid for infrastructure development for economic growth. This included Chinese technical supervision (and at times labor) all at local prices, which enables it to bypass local bureaucracies, and the delays and leakages that often ensue. It also avoids the complex and costly design and bureaucratic implementation processes that have developed in the West.

China also emphasizes, through its Eight Principles, the centrality of

... respect, sovereignty and non-interference, and an insistence on win-win outcomes of South-South development cooperation and mutual opportunity (Mawdsley 2012, 263).

By the 2000s, as the voice of South-South cooperation was increasingly being heard, China was gaining increasing notice, even suggesting a "... fracturing of the Western-dominated aid cartel" (Mawdsley, Savage, and Kim 2014, 29; Kennedy 2010). Its aid program in 2012 was estimated to be $12.5b, or 0.12 percent of GNI; adjusting for per capita income shows that China is one of the most generous aid donors (Lin and Wang 2014). Between 2004–2009 China's aid program grew by nearly 30 percent annually (Bräutigamb 2011, 205). In 2009 it also increased its presence in ASEAN with a major set of announcements which were a mix of aid commercial credits and FDI (Ba 2014). China also wrote off all of its loans made to the least-developed and most heavily indebted countries (Cheng 2010; Cheng and Shi 2009).

China also openly challenged the post-Washington consensus, with what had been referred to as the Beijing Consensus: "equitable growth, positive social change, self-determination, and heavy state control" (Quadir 2013, 326). This approach is based on New Structural Economics, in which the focus moves to countries' endowments and what is lacking, and supporting soft and hard infrastructure plays a large part (Lin 2011; Wang, Ozanne, and Hao 2014).

In addition, China uses a mix of resources and "...freely comingles aid with market-driven inputs such as FDI, imports of raw materials, and export credits" (Hook and Rumsey 2016, 67; Xue 2014). This approach is based on a Chinese adage, "To get rich, first construct a road" (Niu 2016, 208), and "...focuses on the physical infrastructure needed to reduce production and marketing costs" (Wang, Ozanne, and Hao 2014, 52).

Between 2000 and 2010, since the formation of FOCAC, there has been a rapid increase in foreign aid intermingled with FDI to Africa, with FDI increasing tenfold between 2000 and 2012, from $200m to $2.1b (Busse, Erdogan, and Mühlen 2016, 234). Chin estimates that China's total global flow in 2010 was $20–23b, made up of grants, no-interest development loans, as well as lines of concessional financing (Chin 2012, 581). Lin estimated the global aid level component in 2012 to be $12.8b (Lin and Wang 2014, 9).

There is now a more robust voice of the South to challenge the OECD-DAC's post-Washington consensus, to provide clearer airspace for the voice of developing countries (Lim 2015; Renard 2015; Callaghan and Hubbard 2016; Khanna 2014; Solíz 2014), and to move away from neoliberal solutions to a different global world order (Koehler 2015). China has also become more vocal, with Xi Jinping representing a shift away from Deng Xiaoping's so-called "hide and bide" policy—"...hiding one's talents and biding one's time" (Wilson 2015, 1197; Wang and Zeng 2016)—to be more assertive of China's role, to showcase "...the great national rejuvenation and the China Dream" (Godbole 2015, 298). The emphasis is now on more conservative Confucian values and a vision that "emphasises the grandeur and superiority of Chinese culture and civilisation" (Wilson 2015, 1,194).

US Aid Post–Cold War

The US aid program post–Cold War saw some major shifts. The first was to cement a so-called peace dividend with a stronger engagement and possible integration with the US economy, as well as large aid cuts under the Clinton administration (Lai 2003). An important part of this was the move to use the aid program to promote democratization across the former communist world and the developing world more generally. President Clinton referred to the promotion of democracy and human rights as the "third pillar" of his foreign policy (Meernik, Krueger, and Poe 1998, 67; Dunning 2004), and it went hand in hand with liberalized economic growth (Essex 2008).

> The equation of US moral principles with universal ideals, the
> goal of transforming diverse political systems into replications
> of the US model, and the linkage of US material support to ap-
> propriate behaviour by real or potential beneficiaries are deeply
> entrenched features of US foreign policy (Hook 1998, 158).

Despite the high rhetoric there has been little difference in foreign
aid across several administrations on the basis of human rights and
democratization. This may be due to the relative power of Congress
in setting the foreign aid agenda, and bureaucratic inertia (Apodaca
and Stohl 1999; Wang 2016).

The George W. Bush administration made a shift back to the security agenda for foreign aid when it launched the War on Terror
to usher in a new era of unilateralism (Koehler 2015; Moss, Standley, and Roodman 2005; International Institute for Strategic Studies
2001). This harked back to Eisenhower in the 1950s, when he used
foreign aid and military power together. The focus of the War on Terror was on the front-line states and a set of so-called "fragile states"
(Lum 2006). This led to a rapid increase in foreign aid, but little
engagement with China as either an ally or adversary (Woods 2005).
The Obama administration maintained the War on Terror spending,
but returned to more democratic themes with the "…need to in-
vest in building capable, democratic states that can establish healthy
and educated communities, develop markets, and generate wealth"
(Obama 2007, 14). He then went on to add an anti-corruption focus,
as well as continuing the Bush policy of continuing to increase the
aid program, so that between 2002 and 2016 the foreign aid program
(excluding military aid) went from 0.55 percent of budget outlays to
0.85 percent, still a shadow of the 3 percent it was in 1962 (Shapiro
and Weiner 2002; Tarnoff and Lawson 2016).

The 2000s and the Challenge to the Western Aid System

The DAC in the 1960s and 1970s took a more pluralist approach to
foreign aid, reflecting the more state-centered policies of Western Europe. It tended to be less dogmatic about the philosophical direction
foreign aid should take, as the United States had less influence given

its cuts to foreign aid at the time. It was the neoliberal revolution of the 1980s and 1990s, when Western Europe aligned with the neoliberal orthodoxy of the United States and the World Bank in what has become known as the post-Washington consensus, that led to the change in DAC philosophy. However, DAC members such as Japan and South Korea, which have taken a more statist approach to their own development, tend to ignore or remain silent on many of the DAC's neoliberal exhortations (Bräutigam 2011a; Jerve 2007; Jain 2016). Jain argues that Japan in particular has

> ...accommodated Western ideas and DAC norms...but it has consistently foregrounded its own 'self-help' philosophy... to teach the West that models beyond the dominant Western one...should be considered for foreign aid programmes (Jain 2016, 108).

More recently China has been very robust in its critiques of Western aid, particularly the good governance agenda, which it sees as promoting a common institutional form for government (Henderson 2008; Raposo and Potter 2010; Reilly 2012; Wang, Ozanne, and Hao 2014). In negotiations for the DAC-sponsored Accra Agenda for Action of foreign aid principles, China pushed quite hard to insert the clause:

> ...including the principle of non-interference in internal affairs, equality among developing partners and respect for their independence, national sovereignty, cultural diversity and identity and local content (DAC 2008, 4).

This clause sits rather uneasily with other clauses in the Agenda for Action, such as "donors will conduct joint assessments of governance and capacity" (DAC 2008, 5), a reference to post-Washington consensus ideas of what good governance looks like. From China's point of view it is none of the donors' business, and certainly not subject to a joint assessment. By the time the DAC met in Busan four years later in 2011, China's position had hardened further, and Chinese delegates openly questioned "...the universal validity of the claim that democratic ownership, human rights and citizen empowerment are necessary to achieve (economic) development" (Mawdsley, Savage, and Kim 2014, 33), and perhaps led to a shift in the West's position to accommodate China:

> [The] rights-based projection of development effectiveness represented a minority view at Busan, and one that is likely to be overwhelmed by a more dominant growth-centred construction of development effectiveness that appears to be emerging among many DAC and non-DAC states alike (p. 33).

The "growth-centered construction" can be seen with the new Asian Infrastructure Investment Bank (AIIB), which was established in part to challenge the World Bank. Justin Yifu Lin, as the World Bank chief economist, referred to this approach as New Structural Economics, whereby investment is directed by the state to improve "hard and soft infrastructure in order to reduce transaction costs" (Lin 2011, 207). The AIIB has a program of massive investment, together with China's aid and the $40b Silk Road Fund, in the infrastructure of the future, such as the Belt Road Initiative (BRI) to expand both overland and maritime trade links with Europe, Central and South Asia, and Africa. This initiative, like a new Marshall Plan, aims to expand China's economic influence in the broader Eurasian region, as well as employ underemployed Chinese industrial capacity, provide a boost to both the region and China, and help develop a renminbi-centered global financial governance regime (Wei 2016; Li 2015; Lee, Wainwright, and Glassman 2017). BRI may also help avoid a direct confrontation with the United States and Japan in the Pacific, as well as possible conflicts that may emerge with Russia, India, or other powerful states in the region, by providing a range of alternatives to trade with Europe, Asia, and Africa, in addition to the vulnerable South China Sea and Straits of Malacca sea routes.

US Foreign Policy

The other challenge to the United States from China's rapid expansion in foreign aid and FDI lies with US foreign aid policy, which is based on a different paradigm of anti-statism, supporting neoliberal solutions, and building relatively short-term alliances. It is also subject to stringent congressional oversight, which has historically been more skeptical of the strategic benefits to the United States of foreign aid. The Congress does not see foreign aid as a way of "buying" influence in quite the same way that China does. For the US, foreign aid is seen as a short-term tactic in achieving ends such as supporting security allies, gaining votes on the Security Council, protecting Israel in the Middle East, or promoting free market capitalism and therefore new opportunities for US foreign direct investment, rather than directly facilitating it.

China, on the other hand, sees foreign aid in a longer-term strategic sense, as a tool to enhance its status and role in the world: first, in the 1960s, to build relationships with the newly independent states of Africa, whose vote was important in regaining China's seat at the UN and on the Security Council from the Taiwan-based nationalists; and later to show gratitude for their support following sanctions after the Tiananmen Square crackdown (Campbell 2016; Samy 2010; Raposo and Potter 2010; Taylor 1998). Like the US, China seeks a stable and secure world, in which it can build economic linkages that would permit it to more broadly engage in (and benefit from) the economic affairs of the world. China's foreign aid policy also enables the Bretton Woods neoliberal economic orthodoxy, which has been reinforced by the IMF, World Bank, and US government, to be directly challenged (Solíz 2014; Koehler 2015; Sautman and Yan 2007).

> *China's foreign aid policy enables the Bretton Woods neoliberal economic orthodoxy to be directly challenged*

The decline of the West in the face of these strategic challenges poses a problem for the nascent Trump administration. President Trump's proposed aid cuts of around 35 percent follow similar cuts in aid levels in other jurisdictions such as Canada in 2012 and Australia in 2014 (Black 2014; Bhushan 2013; Corbett 2017). While these cuts, in and of themselves, will not have major economic impacts in recipient countries, they can have an effect on the US role in the global marketplace of ideas. Since the 1950s, Western aid programs have been used to varying degrees to promote liberal values, and since the 1980s neoliberal ones. While developing countries have resisted neoliberalism, they have been more open to talking about broader liberal values, at least in their public positioning (Koehler 2015; Solíz 2014). The objections made by the G77 plus China in various fora have not been to the liberal values as expressed through UN resolutions, but the neoliberal economic policies promoted by the West.

The cuts in foreign aid made by a number of US administrations, including those of Johnson, Reagan, and Clinton, were all very large; however, at those times China was not seen as an aid competitor. After the 1970s, it was not until 1989, when the support from Africa was important for rebuilding China's global influence and prestige, that there was a jump in China's foreign aid commitments (Taylor 1998; Muekalia 2004; Huisken 2013). A cut of 35 percent in 2017–2018 to the US aid budget may have a much greater political impact, as China is a larger and more assertive aid donor than it was in the 1980s, now with an expanding program. A pullback by the United States could be a potent signal to China and have implications for North-South relations (Hook and Rumsey 2016). This would also represent a clear step back from Truman's Four Points in terms of global engagement, moving the United States to the position it was in during the interwar years, when it failed to join the League of Nations and generally kept out of world affairs.

The other challenge for the United States is how to engage with the rise of new forms of statism or neocorporatism, which sees a strong state forming alliances, sometimes with dominant religions (e.g., Russia and the Middle East) and big business, and which presents a different kind of threat (Kilby 2015; Shokhin and Kisel 2014). While the United States has traditionally been against statism, the Marshall Plan, the rise in inequality, and the failure of the neoliberal project of the 1980s have led to a rise of state-led national development in many countries, with China, Japan, and South Korea being the most obvious success stories (Yeung 2017). The downside of the rise of the strong state is the erosion of liberal values and notions of liberty that the United States has pushed over time. One example of this is Xi Jinping's exhortation to adopt traditional Confucian values, in contrast to Western liberal ones.

The challenge for the Trump administration is how to use foreign aid to position the United States and its global influence. While the ideas of manifest destiny may have less currency in a more assertive developing world, the leadership that the United States can provide in promoting liberal values and in challenging the rise of illiberal nationalism should not be underestimated. The question is whether that is where Trump wishes to take US aid policy in how it engages with China and South-South relations more broadly. This is particularly so if the "USA first" approach articulated by President Trump becomes policy. Focusing on statism will not work simply because of the success stories of state-led approaches to development and the manifest failure of the neoliberal project. While the Secretary of State has called for a step back on the emphasis on human rights, a broader approach to human rights, which recognizes the right to development as well as economic, social, and cultural rights in its program strategies, should be considered. Any successful engagement with China, however, should be on the basis of mutuality rather than a misplaced sense of moral superiority.

> *Any successful engagement with China should be on the basis of mutuality*

Conclusion

The Bandung Conference was a watershed not only in North-South relations, but in laying the groundwork for a different approach to development cooperation and foreign aid. While the West had steadfastly refused to acknowledge the importance of South-South cooperation and its development following Bandung, the non-aligned movement, the G77, and UNCTAD all left their mark, culminating in the emergence of China's leadership in foreign aid and South-South cooperation in the 2000s. This shift provides a clear challenge to the postwar Western consensus on how developing countries should develop and how they should use foreign aid. It also poses a challenge to the Trump administration and its use of foreign aid in soft diplomacy.

The leadership of China, its approach to providing foreign aid, and the principle on noninterference reduced the West's leverage, in terms of globalization and the broader neoliberal agenda it was promoting in its aid programs. It also weakened the leverage of the West in the broader liberal regime around social justice, gender justice, human rights, environmental norms, and other hard-won global agreements.

This is the challenge for future aid debates, but these will not work if the existing systems led by the US, the World Bank, and the OECD-DAC are to be used, which have either excluded China as an equal partner or implicitly asked China to accept the current Western foreign aid frameworks, or Western-designed norms. While the DAC principles are broadly in line with China's Eight Principles of Foreign Aid, there is still a strong sense of conditionality on aid priorities, and on the best systems of governance a developing country may adopt or move towards. The challenge for the United States and the West is to accept the principle of local sovereignty, and then seek to apply the more globally accepted UN human rights and other norms in those contexts. Over the past 70 years, the United States and China have followed effectively parallel tracks to become major global aid donors. In that time the influence of the United States has been challenged by China, which has used foreign aid to expand its global influence in ways that are quite different to the US. The question is how will the United States respond?

Endnotes

1. The US did provide some foreign aid through the 19th and early part of the 20th century (Liska 1960; Picard and Buss 2009).

2. The other three points of Truman's foreign policy were: support for the UN; world economic recovery including free trade; and the formation of NATO.

3. The Colombo Plan was a North-South initiative and arose from a note about containing communism in a "peaceful way," sent to the British and Australian ambassadors in Beijing in 1949 by the noted Indian historian and diplomat K.M. Panikkar when he was Indian ambassador to China. This idea was then formally taken up at a British Commonwealth ministers' meeting in 1950 held in Colombo, Sri Lanka (Fisher 1971). The US joined the Colombo Plan a year later.

4. The US food aid program was initially a response to the collapse in commodity prices following the Korean War. It then grew rapidly under congressional pressure, which saw it as an effective subsidy to [US] farmers, guaranteed markets, and a way to avoid domestic produce price collapses and the inevitable political backlash (Hagen and Ruttan 1988; Diven 2001; Eggleston 1987).

5. The idea of a Common Aid Effort led to the formation of the Development Assistance Group (DAG) in early 1960 with a primary concern to achieve accurate and comparable data reporting by its Western donor members on their aid flows to developing countries. The idea was that the national-level data would shame the laggards into greater commitments. In 1961 it became the Development Assistance Committee (DAC) under the OECD (Hynes and Scott 2013; White 1974; DAC 1985; Scott 2015).

6. As a sop these concessions were given to Japan.

7. Nehru (India); Ali Khan (Pakistan); Kotelawala (Sri Lanka); Sukarno (Indonesia); and U Nu (Burma).

8. This was an (in)famous phrase in Kipling's pro-colonial poem about the racial superiority of the "white races" in support of US colonialism in the Philippines.

9. Afghanistan, Burma, Cambodia, Ceylon, China, Egypt, Ethiopia, Gold Coast, India, Indonesia, Iran, Iraq, Japan, Jordan, Laos, Lebanon, Liberia, Libya, Nepal, Pakistan, the Philippines, Saudi Arabia, Syria, Sudan, Thailand, Turkey, the Democratic Republic of Vietnam, the State of Vietnam, and the Kingdom of Yemen. Cyprus, though not yet independent, also attended at the invitation of the sponsors. Under pressure from the British colonial government, Joshua Nkrumah of the Gold Coast (now Ghana) withdrew, but other Gold Coast representatives did attend.

10. CENTO, the Central Treaty Organisation made up of Turkey, Iran, Iraq, Pakistan, and the United Kingdom, was also known as the Baghdad Pact; it was dissolved in 1979 following the Iranian revolution and the withdrawal of Iran.

11. This was a compromise reference to the Soviet role in Eastern Europe, as well as Western colonialism, the primary target.

12. Yugoslavia, being part of Europe, was not part of either region.

13. BRICS group of countries made up of Brazil, Russia, India, China, and South Africa.

14. Jack London was an American novelist, journalist, and social activist who shared concerns common among European Americans in California about Asian immigration, described as "the yellow peril"; he used the term as the title of a 1904 essay.

15. According to Westad (2005, 69) Soviet aid to China was 7 percent of Soviet national income from 1953 to 1960, a Soviet Marshall Plan to modernise China, which he argues was the foundation of the Chinese capitalist revolution in the 1980s and 1990s. In this case, however, it was loans rather than grants and had to be paid back. This debt may have had a role in triggering the Sino-Soviet split in 1962 (Chang and Halliday 2007).

16. The risk, as West Germany learned when it set the non-recognition of East Germany as a condition, was that countries would extract more aid using the threat of recognizing the East (White 1974).

17. Organisation of Economic Cooperation and Development (OECD).

18. These were announced in Ghana (Shinn and Eisenman 2012): i) mutual benefit rather than charity; ii) no conditions or privileges for China; iii) interest-free or low-interest loans with the possibility of extending the repayment period if necessary; iv) encouraging independence of the recipient's economy; v) low capital input with quick rates of return; vi) free replacement of unsuitable equipment; vii) "on-the-spot" training of local counterparts; viii) willingness of Chinese experts to accept local living standards.

19. For example, China does not include debt cancellation or university scholarships for study in China in its figures.

20. It was common at the time among many donors to include food aid, which was sold locally with the proceeds used to cover the local costs of projects.

21. UNCTAD and the G77, for a period, prompted a response from Western donors, leading to a reorientation of some foreign aid to address basic human needs and integrated rural development. This was aimed at boosting the livelihoods of the poor who lived mainly in rural areas (Picard and Buss 2009).

Bibliography

Abraham, Itty. 2008. "From Bandung to NAM: Non-alignment and Indian Foreign Policy, 1947–65." *Commonwealth & Comparative Politics* 46 (2): 195–219.

Abraham, Itty. 2014. *How India Became Territorial: Foreign Policy, Diaspora, Geopolitics*. Stanford University Press.

Acharya, Amitav. 1999. "Realism, Institutionalism, and the Asian Economic Crisis." *Contemporary Southeast Asia* 21 (1): 1–29.

Acharya, Amitav. 2016. "Studying the Bandung Conference from a Global IR Perspective." *Australian Journal of International Affairs* 70 (4): 342–357.

Ampiah, Kweku. 2007. *The Political and Moral Imperatives of the Bandung Conference of 1955: The Reactions of the US*. Folkestone, UK: Global Oriental.

Angelo, Anne-Marie, and Tom Adam Davies. 2015. "'American Business Can Assist [African] Hands:' The Kennedy Administration, US Corporations, and the Cold War Struggle for Africa." *The Sixties* 8 (2): 156–178.

Anthony, Ross. 2013. "Infrastructure and Influence: China's Presence on the Coast of East Africa." *Journal of the Indian Ocean Region* 9 (2): 134–149.

Apodaca, Clair, and Michael Stohl. 1999. "United States Human Rights Policy and Foreign Assistance." *International Studies Quarterly* 43 (1): 185–198.

Appadorai, Angadipuram. 1955. *The Bandung Conference*. New Delhi: The Indian Council of World Affairs.

Ashton, Basil, Kenneth Hill, Alan Piazza, and Robin Zeitz. 1994. "Famine in China, 1958–61." *Population and Development Review* 10 (4): 613–645.

Assie-Lumumba, N'Dri Therese. 2015. "Behind and Beyond Bandung: Historical and Forward-looking Reflections on South-South Cooperation." *Bandung: Journal of the Global South* 2: 1–10.

Ba, Alice D. 2014. "Is China Leading? China, Southeast Asia and East Asian Integration." *Political Science* 66 (2): 143–165.

Ban, Cornel, and Mark Blyth. 2013. "The BRICs and the Washington Consensus: An Introduction." *Review of International Political Economy* 20 (2): 241–255.

Bartsch, J.M. 1969a. Memo to Herrenschmidt re: East Block Background Info 65-69 Draft Flow report socialist countries economic aid to less developed countries, October 22. In *OECD Archives* (F18389), edited by OECD. Paris.

Bartsch, J.M. 1969b. East Block Background Info 65-69 Draft Flow Report Socialist Countries Economic Aid to Less Developed Countries Volume, October 26. In *OECD Archives (F18389)*, edited by the OECD. Paris.

Berger, Mark T. 2004. "After the Third World? History, Destiny and the Fate of Third Worldism." *Third World Quarterly* 25 (1): 9–39.

Besada, Hany, and Ben O'Bright. 2017. "Maturing Sino–Africa Relations." *Third World Quarterly* 38 (3): 655–677.

Bhushan, Aniket. 2013. *Foreign Aid and Crises: Examining 2012 Aid Data*: North-South Institute.

Birchall, Ian. 2016. "Capital Of Pariahs." *New Left Review*: 155–160.

Black, David R. 2014. "Humane Internationalism and the Malaise of Canadian Aid Policy." In *Rethinking Canadian Aid,* edited by Stephen Brown, Molly den Heyer, and David R. Black, 17–34. Ottowa: University of Ottawa Press.

Brandt Commission. 1979. Press Release ICIDI (Brandt) Commission on Eighth Meeting July 4–9. In *A1995-357 Brandt Commission Chronological Records 1976–1977,* edited by World Bank. Washington: World Bank Group Archives.

Bräutigam, Deborah. 2011a. "Aid 'With Chinese Characteristics': Chinese Foreign Aid and Development Finance Meet the OECD-DAC Aid Regime." *Journal of International Development* 23 (5): 752–764.

Bräutigam, Deborah. 2011b. "Chinese Development Aid in Africa: What, Where, Why, and How Much?" In *Rising China: Global Challenges and Opportunities,* edited by Jane Golley and Ligang Song. Canberra: ANU Press.

Brazinsky, Gregg A. 2017. *Winning the Third World: Sino-American Rivalry during the Cold War.* UNC Press Books.

Busse, Matthias, Ceren Erdogan, and Henning Mühlen. 2016. "China's Impact on Africa–The Role of Trade, FDI and Aid." *Kyklos* 69 (2): 228–262.

Callaghan, Mike, and Paul Hubbard. 2016. "The Asian Infrastructure Investment Bank: Multilateralism on the Silk Road." *China Economic Journal* 9 (2): 116–139.

Campbell, Austin. 2016. "Riding a Friendly Elephant—How African Nations Can Make the Best of Economic Partnership with China." *Vanderbilt Journal of Transnational Law* 49: 499.

Carrasco, Enrique R. 1999. "The 1980s: The Debt Crisis and the Lost Decade of Development." *Transnational Law and Contemporary Problems* 9: 119.

Carroll, Peter, and William Hynes. 2013. "Engaging with Arab Aid Donors: The DAC Experience." *Institute for International Integration Studies Discussion Papers* 424: 1–19.

Caufield, Catherine. 1996. *Masters of Illusion: The World Bank and the Poverty of Nations.* New York: Henry Holt.

Chang, Jung, and Jon Halliday. 2007. *Mao: The Unknown Story.* New York: Random House.

Cheng, Joseph Y.S. 2016. "Xi Jinping's 'New Model of Major Power Relationships' for Sino-American Relations." *Journal of Comparative Asian Development* 15 (2): 226–254.

Cheng, Joseph Y.S., and Huangao Shi. 2009. "China's African Policy in the Post-Cold War Era." *Journal of Contemporary Asia* 39 (1): 87–115.

Cheng, Yang. 2010. "China Committed to Spirit of Giving." *China Daily,* August 13.

Cheru, Fantu. 2016. "Developing Countries and the Right to Development: A Retrospective and Prospective African View." *Third World Quarterly* 37 (7): 1268–1283.

Chin, Gregory T. 2012. "China as a 'Net Donor': Tracking Dollars and Sense." *Cambridge Review of International Affairs* 25 (4): 579–603.

Clark, William. 1977. Strategy Paper Role of Senior Adviser to Vice President, External Relations, Dec 1. In *McNamara Papers part I:22, Folder 3*, edited by The World Bank. Washington: Library of Congress.

Clemens, Michael A., and Todd J. Moss. 2007. "The Ghost of 0.7 Percent: Origins and Relevance of the International Aid Target." *International Journal of Development Issues* 6 (1): 3–25.

Coles, Roberta L. 2002. "Manifest Destiny Adapted for 1990s War Discourse: Mission and Destiny Intertwined." *Sociology of Religion* 63 (4): 403–426.

Corbett, Jack. 2017. *Australia's Foreign Aid Dilemma: Humanitarian Aspirations Confront Democratic Legitimacy.* London: Routledge.

Crane, Barbara B. 1984. "Policy Coordination by Major Western Powers in Bargaining with the Third World: Debt Relief and the Common Fund." *International Organization* 38 (03): 399–428.

DAC Secretariat. 1964. West Africa Development Problems and External Assistance, Note by the Secretariat for the Regional Meeting on West Africa 14th April. In *OECD Archives DAC(64)30*, edited by OECD. Paris.

DAC Secretariat. 1965. 1965 Development Assistance Efforts and Policies 1965 Review Draft Report by the Chairman July 22. In *OECD Archives DAC(65)58*, edited by OECD. Paris.

DAC Secretariat. 1970. DAC Chairman's Report 14th August. In *OECD Archives (DAC 70-37)*, edited by OECD. Paris.

DAC Secretariat. 1972. DAC Chairman's Report for 1972, 11 Sept. In *OECD Archives (DAC 86.172.72)*, edited by OECD. Paris.

DAC Secretariat. 1973. Chairman's Report 12 Sept 1973. In *OECD Archives (DAC 00.944/73)*, edited by OECD. Paris.

DAC Secretariat. 1978. The Aid Program of China Draft 16th June. In *OECD Archives (DAC F184050 China background information 1979–1980)*, edited by OECD. Paris.

DAC. 1985. *Twenty-Five Years Of Development Co-Operation: A Review Efforts And Policies Of The Members Of The Development Assistance Committee.* Paris: Organisation for Economic Co-operation and Development.

DAC. 2008. Accra Agenda For Action: Third High Level Forum on Aid Effectiveness. Accra, Ghana: DAC.

Dell, Sidney. 1984. "The Emergence of UNCTAD." *IDS Bulletin* 15 (3):7–13.

DeRoche, Andy. 2007. "Non-Alignment on the Racial Frontier: Zambia and the USA, 1964–68." *Cold War History* 7 (2): 227–250.

Diven, Polly J. 2001. "The Domestic Determinants of US Food Aid Policy." *Food Policy* 26 (5): 455–474.

Drabek, Zdenek, and Sam Laird. 1998. "New Liberalism–Trade Policy Developments in Emerging Markets." *The Journal of World Trade* 32: 241–269.

Dreher, Axel, Andreas Fuchs, Bradley Parks, Austin M. Strange, and Michael J. Tierney. 2016. "Apples and Dragon Fruits: The Determinants of Aid and Other Forms of State Financing from China to Africa." University of Heidelberg Department of Economics Discussion Paper Series No. 620.

Dunning, Thad. 2004. "Conditioning the Effects of Aid: Cold War Politics, Donor Credibility, and Democracy in Africa." *International Organization* 58 (02): 409–423.

Eggleston, Robert C. 1987. "Determinants of the Levels and Distribution of PL 480 Food Aid: 1955–1979." *World Development* 15 (6): 797–808.

Engel, Susan. 2012. *The World Bank and the Post-Washington Consensus in Vietnam and Indonesia: Inheritance of Loss.* Routledge.

Enlai, Zhou. 1964. The Chinese Government's Eight Principles for Economic Aid and Technical Assistance to Other Countries January 15. In History and Public Policy Program Digital Archive, (Selected Diplomatic Papers of Zhou Enlai) (Beijing: Zhongyang Wenxian Chubanshe, 1990), 388, edited by Wilson Center Digital Archive. Wilson Center: Wilson Center Digital Archive http://digitalarchive.wilsoncenter.org/document/121560.

Esposito, Chiarella. 1994. *America's Feeble Weapon: Funding the Marshall Plan in France and Italy, 1948–1950.* Westport, CT: Greenwood Publishing Group.

Essex, Jamey. 2008. "The Neoliberalization of Development: Trade Capacity Building and Security at the US Agency for International Development." *Antipode* 40 (2): 229–251.

Evenson, Robert E., and Douglas Gollin. 2003. "Assessing the Impact of the Green Revolution, 1960 to 2000." *Science* 300 (5620): 758–762.

Fisher, Charles A. 1971. "Containing China? II. Concepts and Applications of Containment." *Geographical Journal* 137: 281–310.

Fleck, Robert K., and Christopher Kilby. 2010. "Changing Aid Regimes? US Foreign Aid from the Cold War to the War on Terror." *Journal of Development Economics* 91 (2): 185–197.

Gill, Bates, and Yanzhong Huang. 2006. "Sources and Limits of Chinese 'Soft Power.'" *Survival* 48 (2): 17–36.

Godbole, Avinash. 2015. "China's Asia Strategy under President Xi Jinping." *Strategic Analysis* 39 (3): 298–302.

Goldman, Marshall I. 1967. *Soviet Foreign Aid.* New York: Praeger.

Grant, Richard, and Jan Nijman. 1997. "Historical Changes in U.S. and Japanese Foreign Aid to the Asia–Pacific Region." *Annals of the Association of American Geographers* 87 (1): 32–51.

Griffin, Keith. 1991. "Foreign Aid After the Cold War." *Development and Change* 22 (4): 645–685.

Hagen, James M., and Vernon W. Ruttan. 1988. "Development Policy Under Eisenhower and Kennedy." *The Journal of Developing Areas* 23 (1): 1–30.

Hattori, Tomohisa. 2001. "Reconceptualizing Foreign Aid." *Review of International Political Economy* 8 (4): 633–660.

Henderson, Jeffrey. 2008. "China and Global Development: Towards a Global-Asian Era?" *Contemporary Politics* 14 (4): 375–392.

Higgott, Richard. 1998. "The Asian Economic Crisis: A Study in the Politics of Resentment." *New Political Economy* 3 (3): 333–356.

Hoeffding, Oleg. 1963. "Sino-Soviet Economic Relations, 1959–1962." *The Annals of the American Academy of Political and Social Science* 349 (1): 94–105.

Hongoh, Joseph. 2016. "The Asian-African Conference (Bandung) and Pan-Africanism: The Challenge of Reconciling Continental Solidarity with National Sovereignty." *Australian Journal of International Affairs* 70 (4): 374–390.

Hook, Steven W., and Jessie G. Rumsey. 2016. "The Development Aid Regime at Fifty: Policy Challenges Inside and Out." *International Studies Perspectives* 17 (1): 55–74.

Hook, Steven W. 1998. "'Building Democracy' Through Foreign Aid: The Limitations of United States Political Conditionalities, 1992–96." *Democratization* 5 (3): 156–180.

Howell, Jude, and Jeremy Lind. 2009. *Counter-Terrorism, Aid and Civil Society: Before and After the War on Terror.* Springer.

Huang, Zhengli, and Xiangming Chen. 2016. "Is China Building Africa?" *European Financial Review.* 7.

Huisken, Ron. 2013. *Introducing China: The World's Oldest Great Power Charts Its Next Comeback.* Canberra: ANU Press.

Hynes, William, and Simon Scott. 2013. The Evolution of Official Development Assistance: Achievements, Criticisms and a Way Forward. In *OECD Development Co-operation Working Papers No.12.* Paris: OECD Publishing.

International Institute for Strategic Studies. 2001. "US Foreign Assistance After 11 September." *Strategic Comments* 7 (10): 1–2.

Jain, Purnendra. 2016. "Japan's Foreign Aid: Old and New Contests." *The Pacific Review* 29 (1): 93–113.

Jersild, Austin. 2014. *Sino-Soviet Alliance: An International History.* Chapel Hill, North Carolina: University of North Carolina Press.

Jerve, Alf Morten. 2007. Asian Models for Aid: Is There a Non-Western Approach to Development Assistance? Summary Record of Seminar Held in Oslo, December 2006. In *CMI Report R 2007: 12.* Bergen, Norway: Chr. Michelsen Institute.

Jian, Chen. 2008. "China and the Bandung Conference Changing Perceptions and Representations." In *Bandung Revisited: The Legacy of the 1955 Asian-African Conference for International Order*, edited by Amitav Acharya. Singapore: NUS Press.

Jolly, Richard, Louis Emmerij, Dharam Ghai, and Frédéric Lapeyre. 2004. *UN Contributions to Development Thinking and Practice.* Bloomington: Indiana University Press.

Jones, Matthew. 2005. "A 'Segregated' Asia?: Race, the Bandung Conference, and Pan-Asianist Fears in American Thought and Policy, 1954–1955." *Diplomatic History* 29 (5): 841–868.

Kawamura, Noriko. 1997. "Wilsonian Idealism and Japanese Claims at the Paris Peace Conference." *Pacific Historical Review* 66 (4): 503–526.

Kennedy, John F. 1961. Address by President John F. Kennedy to the UN General Assembly, September 25, 1961. In *Diplomacy in Action*, edited by U.S. Department of State. Washington: U.S. Department of State

Kennedy, John F. 1962. "Foreign Aid 1961: Selections from the Message of the President to Congress March 22, 1961." In *Why Foreign Aid?*, edited by Robert A. Goldwin. Chicago: Rand McNally.

Kennedy, Scott. 2010. "The Myth of the Beijing Consensus." *Journal of Contemporary China* 19 (65): 461–477.

Khanna, Parag. 2014. "New BRICS Bank a Building Block of Alternative World Order." *New Perspectives Quarterly* 31 (4): 46–48.

Kilby, Patrick. 2015. *NGOs and Political Change: A History of the Australian Council for International Development.* Canberra: ANU Press.

Kipling, Rudyard, and Charles Wolcott Balestier. 1899. *Departmental Ditties: Barrack-Room Ballads and Other Verses. The Five Nations. The Seven Seas.* Vol. 2. New York: Doubleday, Page and Company, 1925.

Kitano, Naohiro. 2014. "China's Foreign Aid at a Transitional Stage." *Asian Economic Policy Review* 9 (2): 301–317.

Koehler, Gabriele. 2015. "Seven Decades of 'Development,' and Now What?" *Journal of International Development* 27 (6): 733–751.

Koslowski, Rey, and Friedrich V. Kratochwil. 1994. "Understanding Change in International Politics: The Soviet Empire's Demise and the International System." *International Organization* 48 (02): 215–247.

Kunz, Diane B. 1997. "The Marshall Plan Reconsidered: A Complex of Motives." *Foreign Affairs* 76 (3): 162–170.

Kyle, Keith. 1991. *Suez: Britain's End of Empire in the Middle East.* New York: IB Tauris.

Labouisse, Henry R. 1961. An Act for International Development, A Program for the Decade of Development: Summary Presentation, June 1961. In *General Foreign Policy Series 169*, edited by Department of State Publication 7205. Washington, DC: US Government Printing Office.

Lai, Brian. 2003. "Examining the Goals of US Foreign Assistance in the Post-Cold War Period, 1991–96." *Journal of Peace Research* 40 (1): 103–128.

Lancaster, Carol. 2008. *Foreign Aid: Diplomacy, Development, Domestic Politics.* University of Chicago Press.

Larkin, Bruce D. 1973. *China and Africa, 1949–1970: The Foreign Policy of the People's Republic of China.* Berkeley: Univ. of California Press.

Lavelle, Kathryn C. 2013. American Politics, the Presidency of the World Bank, and Development Policy. In *Policy Research Working Paper WPS6377.* Washington: World Bank Group Archives.

Lee, Seung-Ook, Joel Wainwright, and Jim Glassman. 2017. "Geopolitical Economy and the Production of Territory: The Case of US–China Geopolitical-Economic Competition in Asia." *Environment and Planning A*:0308518X17701727.

Lees, Lorraine M. 1978. "The American Decision to Assist Tito, 1948–1949." *Diplomatic History* 2 (4): 407–422.

Li, Mingjiang. 2015. "China's 'One Belt, One Road' Initiative: New Round of Opening Up." *RSIS Commentary* 50 (March).

Lim, Alvin Cheng-Hin. 2015. "The US, China and the AIIB: From Zero-Sum Competition to Win-Win Cooperation?" *Eurasia Review*, April 19.

Lin, Justin Yifu. 2011. "New Structural Economics: A Framework for Rethinking Development." *The World Bank Research Observer* 26 (2): 193–221.

Lin, Justin Yifu, and Yan Wang. 2014. China-Africa Co-operation in Structural Transformation: Ideas, Opportunities, and Finances. WIDER Working Paper.

Liska, George. 1960. *The New Statecraft: Foreign Aid in American Foreign Policy*. Chicago: University of Chicago Press.

Loayza, Matthew. 2003. "An 'Aladdin's Lamp' for Free Enterprise: Eisenhower, Fiscal Conservatism, and Latin American Nationalism, 1953–61." *Diplomacy & Statecraft* 14 (3): 83–105.

Lum, Thomas. 2006. US Foreign Aid to East and South Asia: Selected Recipients. In *CRS Report for Congress*. Washington: Congressional Research Service: The Library of Congress.

Maddux, John L. 1981. *The Development Philosophy of Robert S. McNamara*. Washington: World Bank.

Mattlin, Mikael, and Matti Nojonen. 2015. "Conditionality and Path Dependence in Chinese Lending." *Journal of Contemporary China* 24 (94): 701–720.

Maurice, Williams. 1975. 1975 review. Report by the Chairman. Development Co-operation: Efforts and Policies of the Members of the DAC. In *OECD Archives (DAC I-22/79P(E)2)*, edited by OECD. Paris.

Mawdsley, Emma. 2012. "The Changing Geographies of Foreign Aid and Development Cooperation: Contributions from Gift Theory." *Transactions of the Institute of British Geographers* 37 (2): 256–272.

Mawdsley, Emma, Laura Savage, and Sung-Mi Kim. 2014. "A 'Post-aid World'? Paradigm Shift in Foreign Aid and Development Cooperation at the 2011 Busan High Level Forum." *The Geographical Journal* 180 (1): 27–38.

Meernik, James, Eric L. Krueger, and Steven C. Poe. 1998. "Testing Models of US Foreign Policy: Foreign Aid During and After the Cold War." *The Journal of Politics* 60 (1): 63–85.

Miles, Caroline. 1968. "UNCTAD: Prospects for the New Delhi Session." *The World Today* 24 (2): 64–71.

Monson, Jamie. 2006. "Defending the People's Railway in the Era of Liberalization: TAZARA in Southern Tanzania." *Africa* 76 (01): 113–130.

Monson, Jamie. 2013. "Remembering Work on the Tazara Railway in Africa and China, 1965–2011: When 'New Men' Grow Old." *African Studies Review* 56 (01): 45–64.

Morgan, John. 2001. *Development, Globalisation and Sustainability.* Cheltenham, UK: Nelson Thornes.

Morley, Lorna, and Felix Muskett Morley. 1961. *The Patchwork History of Foreign Aid.* Washington: American Enterprise Association.

Morrison, David R. 1998. *Aid and Ebb Tide: A History of CIDA and Canadian Development Assistance.* Waterloo, ON: Wilfrid Laurier Univ. Press.

Moss, Todd J., Scott Standley, and David Roodman. 2005. "The Global War on Terror and US Development Assistance: USAID Allocation by Country, 1998–2005." Working Paper 62. Center for Global Development.

Muekalia, Domingos Jardo. 2004. "Africa and China's Strategic Partnership." *African Security Studies* 13 (1): 5–11.

Narayanan, K.R. 2004. "The 50th Anniversary of Panchsheel." *Chinese Journal of International Law* 3: 369.

Nesadurai, Helen. 2008. "Bandung and the Political Economy of North South Relations: Sowing the Seeds for Revisioning International Society." In *Bandung Revisited: The Legacy of the 1955 Asian-African Conference for International Order*, edited by Amitav Acharya. Singapore: NUS Press.

Niu, Zhongguang. 2016. "China's Development and its Aid Presence in Africa: A Critical Reflection from the Perspective of Development Anthropology." *Journal of Asian and African Studies* 51 (2): 199–221.

Obama, Barack. 2007. "Renewing American Leadership." *Foreign Affairs*: 2–16.

ODI. 1980. Briefing Paper no 2 March. The Brandt Commission. In *A1995-357 Brandt Commission Chronological Records 1976–1977;* edited by The World Bank. Washington: World Bank Group.

OECD-DAC. 1979. The Aid Program of China Draft: 16th June 1978. In *F184050 OECD Archives* edited by OECD. Paris.

Orr, Robert M. 1988. "The Aid Factor in US-Japan Relations." *Asian Survey* 28 (7): 740–756.

Parker, Guy. 1956. Bandung in Perspective. In *Centre for International Studies*, edited by Amitav Acharya. Cambridge (Mass.): MIT.

Parker, Jason. 2006. "Cold War II: The Eisenhower Administration, the Bandung Conference, and the Reperiodization of the Postwar Era." *Diplomatic History* 30 (5): 867–892.

Patel, Raj. 2013. "The Long Green Revolution." *The Journal of Peasant Studies* 40 (1): 1–63.

Picard, Louis A., and Terry F. Buss. 2009. *A Fragile Balance: Re-examining the History of Foreign Aid, Security, and Diplomacy.* Sterling, VA: Kumarian Press.

Quadir, Fahimul. 2013. "Rising Donors and the New Narrative of 'South–South' Cooperation: What Prospects for Changing the Landscape of Development Assistance Programmes?" *Third World Quarterly* 34 (2): 321–338.

Raposo, Pedro Amakasu, and David M. Potter. 2010. "Chinese and Japanese Development Co-operation: South–South, North–South, or What?" *Journal of Contemporary African Studies* 28 (2): 177–202.

Reilly, James. 2012. "A Norm-Taker or a Norm-Maker? Chinese Aid in Southeast Asia." *Journal of Contemporary China* 21 (73): 71–91.

Renard, Thomas. 2015. "The Asian Infrastructure Investment Bank (AIIB): China's New Multilateralism and the Erosion of the West." *Security Policy Brief No. 63.*

Republic of Indonesia. 1955. Final Communiqué of the Asian-African Conference of Bandung (24 April 1955). Bandung: The Ministry of Foreign Affairs, Republic of Indonesia.

Samy, Yiagadeesen. 2010. "China's Aid Policies in Africa: Opportunities and Challenges." *The Round Table* 99 (406): 75–90.

Sautman, Barry, and Hairong Yan. 2007. "Friends and Interests: China's Distinctive Links with Africa." *African Studies Review* 50 (3): 75–114.

Scott, Simon. 2015. The Accidental Birth of "Official Development Assistance." In *OECD Development Co-Operation Working Paper 24.* Paris: OECD.

Shapiro, Isaac, and David Weiner. 2002. "Still Not Enough Aid." *Challenge* 45 (4): 60–70.

Shen, Simon, and Cho-kiu Li. 2015. "The Cultural Side-Effects of the Sino-Soviet Split: The Influence of Albanian Movies in China in the 1960s." *Modern China Studies* 22 (1): 215.

Shinn, David H., and Joshua Eisenman. 2012. *China and Africa: A Century of Engagement.* Philadelphia: University of Pennsylvania Press.

Shokhin, Alexander, and Kirill Kisel. 2014. "Modern Models Of Interaction Between Business And Government In Russia: Corporatism Or Pluralism?" Higher School of Economics Research Paper No. WP BRP 14/PS/2014.

Solíz, Llorentty. 2014. Declaration of the Summit of Heads of State and Government of the Group of 77 For a New World Order for Living Well, Santa Cruz de la Sierra, Plurinational State of Bolivia, 14 and 15 June 2014; Annex to the letter dated 7 July 2014 from the Permanent Representative of the Plurinational State of Bolivia to the United Nations, addressed to the Secretary-General, edited by United Nations General Assembly. New York: UNGA.

Song, Wei. 2015. "Seeking New Allies in Africa: China's Policy Towards Africa During the Cold War as Reflected in the Construction of the Tanzania–Zambia Railway." *Journal of Modern Chinese History* 9 (1): 46–65. doi: 10.1080/17535654.2015.1030836.

Strand, Jonathan R., Eduardo M. Flores, and Michael W. Trevathan. 2016. "China's Leadership in Global Economic Governance and the Creation of the Asian Infrastructure Investment Bank." *Rising Powers Quarterly* 1 (1): 55–69.

Suehiro, Akira. 1999. "The Road to Economic Re-entry: Japan's Policy Toward Southeast Asian Development in the 1950s and 1960s." *Social Science Japan Journal* 2 (1): 85–105.

Tansky, Leo. 1967. "US and USSR Aid to Developing Countries: A Comparative Study of India, Turkey, and the UAR." New York: Praeger.

Tarnoff, Curt, and Marian L. Lawson. 2016. Foreign Aid: An Introduction to U.S. Programs and Policy, June 17. In *Congressional Research Service 7-5700 R40213*. Washington: US Congress.

Taylor, Ian. 1998. "China's Foreign Policy Towards Africa in the 1990s." *The Journal of Modern African Studies* 36 (03): 443–460.

United States Congress, ed. 1957a. *Study no1 The Objectives of The United States Economic Assistance Programs*. Edited by United States Congress Senate Special Committee to Study the Foreign Aid Program. *The Foreign Aid Program: Compilation of Studies and Surveys / prepared under the direction of the Special Committee to Study the Foreign Aid Program, United States Senate, pursuant to S.Res.285, 84th Congress, and S.Res.35 and 141, 85th Congress*. Washington: United States Congress.

United States Congress. 1957b. "Senate, 'The Objectives of United States Economic Assistance Programs,' prepared under the direction of The Special Committee to Study the Foreign Aid Program." In *Foreign Aid Program: Compilation of Studies and Surveys, 85th Cong., 1st sess.*, 4–6. Washington: United States Government Printing Office.

Varrall, Merriden. 2016. "Domestic Actors and Agendas in Chinese Aid Policy." *The Pacific Review* 29 (1): 21–44.

Verschaeve, Joren, and Jan Orbie. 2015a. "Once a Member, Always a Member? Assessing the Importance of Time in the Relationship Between the European Union and the Development Assistance Committee." *Cambridge Review of International Affairs*: 1–16.

Verschaeve, Joren, and Jan Orbie. 2015b. "The DAC is Dead, Long Live the DCF? A Comparative Analysis of the OECD Development Assistance Committee and the UN Development Cooperation Forum." *European Journal of Development Research* advanced online May 2015: 1–17.

Vieira, Marco A. 2016. "Understanding Resilience in International Relations: The Non-Aligned Movement and Ontological Security." *International Studies Review* 18 (2): 290–311.

Wang, Yu. 2016. "The Effect of Bargaining on US Economic Aid." *International Interactions* 42 (3): 479–502.

Wang, Xiaobing, Adam Ozanne, and Xin Hao. 2014. "The West's Aid Dilemma and the Chinese Solution?" *Journal of Chinese Economic and Business Studies* 12 (1): 47–61.

Wang, Zhengxu, and Jinghan Zeng. 2016. "Xi Jinping: The Game Changer of Chinese Elite Politics?" *Contemporary Politics* 22 (4): 469–486. doi: 10.1080/13569775.2016.1175098.

Wei, Shen. 2016. "Rising Renminbi and the Neo-Global Financial Governance in the Context of 'One Belt One Road' Initiative: A Changing Game or Minor Supplement?" *Journal of International Banking Law and Regulation* 32 (1): 10–21.

Westad, Odd Arne. 2005. *The Global Cold War: Third World Interventions and the Making of our Times.* Cambridge: Cambridge University Press.

White, John. 1974. *The Politics of Foreign Aid.* London and Toronto: Bodley Head.

Wilson, Jeanne L. 2015. "Soft Power: A Comparison of Discourse and Practice in Russia and China." *Europe-Asia Studies* 67 (8): 1171–1202. doi: 10.1080/09668136.2015.1078108.

Wood, Robert Everett. 1986. *From Marshall Plan to Debt Crisis: Foreign Aid and Development Choices in the World Economy.* Vol. 355. Berkeley and Los Angeles: Univ. of California Press.

Woods, Ngaire. 2005. "The Shifting Politics of Foreign Aid." *International Affairs* 81 (2): 393–409.

Woods, Ngaire. 2008. "Whose Aid? Whose Influence? China, Emerging Donors and the Silent Revolution in Development Assistance." *International Affairs* 84 (6): 1205–1221.

World Bank. 1982a. Memo: ul Haq to Clausen Feb 8, China Major Policy Issues. In *Country Files China A A1990-013 1774658*, edited by The World Bank. Washington: World Bank Group Archives.

World Bank. 1982b. Vergin to Clausen Feb 10: China CPP: Country Program issues. In *Country Files China A A1990-013 1774658*, edited by The World Bank. Washington: World Bank Group Archives.

World Bank. 1983. Koch Weser to file May 5 Clausen's meeting with Li Peng Vice Minister of Finance. In *Country Files China A A1990-013 1774658*, edited by The World Bank. Washington: World Bank Group Archives.

World Bank. 1985. Memo: from Katz on the Discussion Draft of China Paper 25 Sept. In *A1994-022#42* edited by World Bank. Washington: World Bank Group Archives.

Wright, Richard. 1956. *The Color Curtain: A Report on the Bandung Conference.* Cleveland, OH: The World Publishing Company.

Xue, Lan. 2014. "China's Foreign Aid Policy and Architecture." *IDS Bulletin* 45 (4): 36–45.

Yeh, Emily T., and Elizabeth Wharton. 2016. "Going West and Going Out: Discourses, Migrants, and Models in Chinese Development." *Eurasian Geography and Economics* 57 (3): 286–315.

Yeung, Henry Wai-Chung. 2017. "Rethinking the East Asian Developmental State in its Historical Context: Finance, Geopolitics and Bureaucracy." *Area Development and Policy* 2 (1): 1–23.

Zoysa, Richard de. 2005. "America's Foreign Policy: Manifest Destiny or Great Satan?" *Contemporary Politics* 11 (2–3): 133–156.

Acknowledgments

The research for this study was supported by an East-West Center Asia Studies Fellowship. I would like to thank the staff at the East-West Center in Washington office and in particular Satu Limaye and Grace Ruch Clegg for their encouragement and support, as well as the helpful comments from a seminar at the East-West Center in May 2017. Thanks to the series editors Dieter Ernst and Marcus Mietzner, and anonymous reviewers who commented on earlier drafts. Special thanks to my partner Dr. Joyce Wu for her encouragement and support, and her forbearance on my long absence from home.

www.ingramcontent.com/pod-product-compliance
Lightning Source LLC
Chambersburg PA
CBHW071341290326
41933CB00040B/2036